Imagination

Imagination

Compiled by
Marlene Peterson

Well-Educated Mother's Heart Learning Library
Libraries of Hope

Imagination

The Training of the Imagination, by James Rhoades, London: John Lane Co., (1908).

Education Through Imagination, by Margaret McMillan, London: Swan Sonnenschein & Co., (1904).

Libraries of Hope, Inc.
Appomattox, Virginia 24522

Website www.librariesofhope.com
Email support@librariesofhope.com

Printed in the United States of America

Table of Contents

Imagination

The Dreamers

They are the architects of greatness. Their vision lies within their souls. They never see the mirages of Fact, but peer beyond the veils and mists of doubt and pierce the walls of unborn Time.

The world has accoladed them with jeer and sneer and jibe, for worlds are made of little men who take but never give–who share but never spare–who cheer a grudge and grudge a cheer.

Wherefore, the paths of progress have been sobs of blood dropped from their broken hearts.

Makers of empire, they have fought for bigger things than crowns and higher seats than thrones. Fanfare and pageant and the right to rule or will to love, are not the fires which wrought their resolution into steel.

Grief only streaks their hair with silver, but has never grayed their hopes.

They are the Argonauts, the seekers of the priceless fleece–the Truth.

Through all the ages they have heard the voice of destiny call to them from the unknown vasts. They dare uncharted seas, for they are makers of the charts. With only cloth of courage at their masts and with no compass save their dreams, they sail away undaunted for the far, blind shores.

Their brains have wrought all human miracles. In lace of stone their spires stab the Old World's skies and with their golden crosses kiss the sun.

The belted wheel, the trail of steel, the churning screw, are shuttles in the loom on which they weave their magic tapestries.

A flash out in the night leaps leagues of snarling seas and cries to shore for help, which, but for one man's dream, would never come.

Their tunnels plow the river-bed and chain the islands to the Motherland.

Their wings of canvas beat the air and add the highways of the eagle to the human paths.

A God-hewn voice swells from a disc of glue and wells out through a throat of brass, caught sweet and whole, to last beyond the maker of the song, because a dreamer dreamt.

What would you have of fancy or of fact if hands were all with which men had to build?

Your homes are set upon the land a dreamer found. The pictures on its walls are visions from a dreamer's soul. A dreamer's pain wails from your violin.

They are the chosen few–the Blazers of the way–who never wear doubt's bandage on their eyes–who starve and chill and hurt, but hold to courage and to hope, because they know that there is always proof of truth for them who try–that only cowardice and lack of faith can keep the seeker from his chosen goal, but if his heart be strong and if he dream enough and dream it hard enough, he can attain, no matter where men failed before.

Walls crumble and the empires fall. The tidal wave sweeps from the sea and tears a fortress from its rocks. The rotting nations drop from off Time's bough, and only things the dreamers make live on.

They are the Eternal Conquerors–their vassals are the years.

– Herbert Kaufman

Imagination and Fairy Tales

Frances Jenkins Olcott (*The Children's Reading*):

"Imagination is the faculty that brings the soul into most immediate contact with ideas, feelings, or objects, and with other minds or beings."—Curry.

"Through imaginative literature abstract truths are made to have for the child a reality which is given to them by the experiences of daily life only by the slowest degrees."—Bates.

"I do not like to read lies to my child," is the verdict of many a mother. "I give him only histories, biographies, and useful books." She does not know, this really earnest mother, that she is shutting the door of her child's imagination, and that she may be hampering his power to do great things in after life, by thus closing to him the storehouse of imaginative literature. For later he will not be able to draw full sustenance from classic writings unless he has been fed in youth on the best of folk-literature.

The action of the picture-making power of the mind—the imagination—is a part of almost every mental process. The act of memory calls up mental pictures, the act of fancy re-creates a world, invention, writing, painting, and conceiving a scientific theory are aided by the creative imagination. And, what is more, the sympathetic feelings, of charity, compassion, and the power to put one's self in the place of another, are dependent on the movement of the same faculty.

Tyndall gives most impressive testimony to the value of the applied use of the imagination. "There are Tories," he writes, "even in science, who regard imagination as a faculty to be feared and avoided rather than employed. They have observed its action in weak vessels, and are unduly impressed with its disasters. But they might with equal justice point to exploded boilers as an argument against the use of steam. With accurate experiment and observation to work upon, imagination becomes the architect of physical theory. Newton's passage from a falling apple to a falling moon, was an act of the prepared imagination, without which the laws of Kepler could never have been traced to their foundations. Out of the facts of chemistry the constructive imagination of Dalton formed the atomic theory. Davy was richly endowed with the imaginative faculty, while with Faraday its exercise was incessant, preceding, accompanying, and guiding all his experiments. His strength and fertility as a discoverer is to be referred in great part to the stimulus of his imagination."

Thus imagination is a most powerful factor in daily life, and to develop in the individual a wholesome and rich imagination, and to correlate it with the reason, is of utmost importance. This can be best accomplished in childhood. For the didactic faculty—the reason—is dormant in a child, and the faculty of pure enjoyment—the imagination—is predominant, and is the open door to his mind. Through it enters a constant procession of mental pictures, each making an impression on the plastic brain, where they are stored away until the day comes when the mind, at will, recalls the images and with them recombines and forms original designs.

One of the surest means of educating the imagination is through the judicious use of the best literature which will enrich and stimulate the picture-making faculty. Let us now see how fables, myths, folk and wonder tales will aid this development.

Folk-literature conserves the accumulating mass of spontaneous, unscientific thought, feelings, beliefs, fancies, traditions, distortions, superstitions, and ethical teachings of the common people of all races. It has no known authors, but, like an avalanche, it gathers into itself, age by age, all that lies in its path of the natural mental products of the human race. In treatment it is imaginative, and objective—in fact, childlike. It has, however, a two-fold nature. It teaches, on the one hand, simple truths and morals, put in a way that appeals directly to children; it also shows the distinction between elemental good and evil; and that retribution follows sin; and it emphasizes the majesty or beauty of nature. While on the other hand, there runs throughout folk-literature a strain of illogicality, and immorality—called by some folk-lorists the irrational—which contradicts the ethical teachings. But when this illogical, irrational element is eliminated, there yet remains a vast body of folk-literature, rich in those qualities that build up and stimulate the imagination, and inculcate simple virtues within the understanding of children.

Folk-literature for children divides itself roughly into seven groups: fables, pure myths, hero-myths, place-legends, fairy-lore, nursery tales and rhymes, and hero-romances. The rhymes and romances will be discussed in another chapter.

The beast-fable appears to be one of the earliest forms of story-telling among all peoples. The savage races use it as a means of teaching mythical tribal history, as well as for entertainment. The savage beast-fable and short story of Africa and Australia are of a low order of imagination, distorted, and full of deceit, lying, and brutality, presented in such a way that children cannot fail to derive wrong ethical ideas therefrom; whereas the Hindus, Greeks, and other Indo-Germanic peoples have turned the beast-fable into a vehicle for the teaching of homely virtues and worldly wisdom of a practical kind. Many of these fables have become an integral part of our literature, and if for no other reason children should be made familiar with them. They have, however, a special mission in the ethical education of children. They not only please the fancy, but they satisfy a young child's craving for short, objective, moral tales, and they inculcate such virtues as prudence, foresight, honesty, and homely wisdom. Fables that teach revenge, and overcoming by the means of craft, should be rejected from books for children. Some of the best Æsopic fables to tell or read are "Belling the Cat," "The Dog in the Manger," "The Lion and the Mouse," "The Shepherd Boy and the Wolf," and "The Town and Country Mouse."

Pure myths had their origin in primitive man's interpretation of nature. The rising and setting of the sun, the return of spring after the winter, the stars in the heavens, the storms and the winds and the loud-sounding Ocean, all filled him with wonderment and awe. He expressed his understanding of natural phenomena in poetic imagery and language, which came, in time, to be believed as religion. The first form of myth, says Ruskin, "contains the germ of accomplished tradition; but only as the seed contains the flower. As the intelligence and passion of the race develop, they cling to and nourish their beloved and sacred legend; leaf by leaf it expands under the touch of pure affections, and more delicate imagination, until at last the perfect fable bourgeons out into symmetry of milky stem and honied bell."

Of such myths the best types are found in Greek mythology. Harmony, poetic feeling for the beauties of nature, personification of the gentle and tender side of nature make this mythology enjoyable to little children, who love stories of flowers, trees, and living things, fountains, and sudden transformations; of such stories the best types are Arachne, Daphne, Arethusa, Echo and Narcissus, Phaethon, Pygmalion and Galatea, and Proserpine. Each Greek myth is complete in itself, and is not dependent on another tale to show forth an inner meaning. This again makes the Greek myth peculiarly applicable to little children who desire a complete story in a few words.

Thus, as each Greek myth is gracefully complete in itself, and usually presents an aesthetic idea in poetic form; so, on the other hand, the Norse myth is a part of a complicated system of creation, according to Germanic tradition. Its gods are personifications of the stupendous, awe-inspiring natural phenomena of the North. The cold "long nights" followed by brief hot summers, and the struggle for existence in the face of violent elements, have left their impress on the mythological system of the people. The thunder of the storm on the mountains, the rush of the avalanche, the beat of seas on rocky coasts, the lapping of the waves of the fiords, the mysterious play of the Northern lights, have united in producing a vigorous, epic-like mythology, replete with manly courage and stalwart virtues, but permeated with a mystic melancholy, so characteristic of the people of the North; of whom Carlyle says: "I feel that these old Northmen were looking into nature with open eye and soul; most earnest, honest, childlike; and yet manlike; with a great-hearted simplicity and depth and freshness, in a true, loving, admiring, unfearing way. A right valiant, true old race of men."

These Norse myths have, therefore, a positive mission in the education of Anglo-Saxon-thinking children. Stripped of their grosser parts, the myths present a united group of tales emphasizing Germanic ideas of unity, individual liberty, of right and wrong, of courage and manliness. These qualities are drawn with strong strokes, and painted in contrasting colors; virtue is virtue, badness is badness, there are no shades of coloring. The stories please the wonder-loving children because they tell of the adventures of gods and goddesses, and of frost-giants, light-elves, and elves of darkness, of trolls, and hideous monsters, as well as of mighty heroes and splendid women.

Another mythology that has a place in the education of children is that of the American Indian.

It breathes of the nature of the wild woods; it is reverent and mystical. On the other hand, it is in part fierce, illogical, confused; especially so when relating the origin of tribes and families. Very little satisfactory work has been done in rendering these tales for children. Longfellow's "Hiawatha" still occupies the important place of presenting in the best form, though idealized, the poetic side of Indian mythology.

There are many other mythologies, but none that offers, as far as the writer knows, such concrete educational characteristics as do the Greek, Old Norse, and Red Indian.

We may now pass on to the brief consideration of the hero-myth. The Norse mythology is a combination of pure myth and hero-worship, probably founded upon the historic traditions of tribal heroes, as well as on nature-worship. The story of Sigurd the Volsung's son will be considered later in the chapter on "Ballads, Epics, and Romances." The Greeks were rich in hero-stories, such as those of Hercules and of Theseus, Perseus and Jason. The adventures of the last three heroes are delightfully told for children by Hawthorne in his graceful, inimitable style; while Kingsley has treated the same tales with a nearer approach to their classical originals.

The place-legend is an imaginative accessory to history, and is the outcome of the fancy and superstition of the common people, who weave fearsome or poetic tales about their local towns, castles, rocks, mountains, trees, or abandoned houses, and other objects. Of this class are the tales of William Tell, Rip Van Winkle, the Lorelei, Ulysses's sirens, Tannhauser, and many other tales, some of which deal with ghosts, banshees, wild huntsmen, and other morbid superstitions not wholesome for all children.

Fairy-lore is largely the product of the Celtic mind, which is fanciful and poetic. The best stories of this kind may be found in English, Scottish, and Irish folk-lore. They deal with the doings of "the little people," with fairy-rings, moonlight dances, enchanted mountains, changelings, maidens and youths decoyed to Fairy-Land, and with imps and elves that "give pinches, nips, and bobs" to bad folk, and with King Oberon, Queen Titania, and merry, freakish Robin Goodfellow.

We pass now to the ever popular nursery tale—the myth or folk-tale recast and told by "old gammers" to the little ones. Here appear classic myths in new garments, Cupid and Psyche masquerading as Beauty and the Beast, and, in the Scandinavian version, as the maiden and the "great big white bear" of East of the Sun and West of the Moon; while Orpheus and Eurydice reappear in the land of the Red Indian, where the bereaved husband follows his Indian wife to the Land of Souls. The Valkyrie, Brynhild, aroused by Sigurd from her sleep-thorn slumber, is transformed in the nursery into the Sleeping Beauty waking at the kiss of "a fairy prince, with joyful eyes, and lighter-footed than the fox." The Barbe Bleue of the Breton place-legend becomes Blue Beard; and a possible Cornish hero in the wars with the Romans, invades the nursery as Jack the Giant Killer; and, with a lack of dignity not to be explained by the scale of divine ascension to the Buddhaship, Buddha transmigrates from the son of King Brahmadatta, and reappears in Brer Rabbit, and the Demon with the Matted Hair becomes the wonderful Tar Baby.

Cinderella teaches the reward of modesty and humility, as do a host of other nursery tales; Toads and Diamonds, the reward of charity and a kind heart; Faithful John, friendship and loyalty even unto death; and the Little House in the Wood, kindness to animals. Accumulative tales satisfy the ear as well as the fancy, and the "drolls" and grotesque tales are a never ending source of delight.

Unfortunately, many nursery tales included in collections for children present perverted ideas of right, the themes of which are success by craft, lying, and theft; and they also justify ingratitude, disloyalty, and irreverence. These stories should be cast out of collections for children. Even some of the ancients did not believe in telling or reading to little ones such irrational tales. Such stories, says Plato, "ought not to be lightly told to young and simple persons....Poets and story-tellers make the gravest misstatements about men when they say that many wicked men are happy, and good men miserable; and we shall forbid them to utter such things."

Nursery tales need careful editing. But there is no more delicate task than to handle folk-literature with the respect that will preserve for the children its directness of appeal, its colloquial language, its humor and grotesqueness, the swift action of plots, the rewards and retributions that are dealt out, *without moralizing*, and, what is more, the destruction, swift and awful, which overtakes ravenous dragons, evil witches and trolls, and fearsome ogres and giants. Fine examples of this folk-treatment in rendering nursery tales may be found in any good translation of Grimm, also in Joseph Jacobs's volumes of fairy tales, and in Ernest Rhys's "Fairy-Gold."

Some editors, in their over-zeal to make folk-tales mediums of moral instruction, lose their own sense of humor and their perspective. An example of this treatment may be found in a certain version of "The Three Bears"—the little tale attributed to Southey, but which has become a part of nursery literature. The editor adds a good deal of sentimental detail not included in the accepted version. She interlards her tale with remarks like the following: "That is the polite way children talk to animals. Animals like it." "Where were the bears all this time that they did not come in to shake hands with their little visitor?" and at that dramatic moment—which every child awaits with breathless suspense—when the little bear discovers Goldilocks asleep in his bed, the little bear of this version laughs, and strokes the child's golden hair, chivalrously offering his paw to help her rise, while the great, huge bear hides his paws behind him, "so the child should not be scared." "I beg your pardon, Mr. and Mrs. Bear," says the polite child, "I will never do so again," and distributing checkerberries, she invites the bears to call upon her, then runs home.

And what does any child get from such a mawkish tale—from which all the vigor of the original has been stripped? Where is the little listener's blissful anticipation of the final sympathetic thrill at the end—to which the whole story leads up? "Somebody has been lying in my bed," cries the little bear; *"And here she is!!"* And Goldilocks wakes in fright, jumps out the open window, and runs home as fast as her legs can carry her. And, what is more, where is the editor's sense of humor, when she can so render a tale and write in the preface to the same book: "The youngest children are at one with birds, beasts, and insects, and it is only through imitation and instruction that they learn to avoid these creatures." To be consistent with this, the writer should certainly teach modern children to avoid "bear hugs" and by scaring them thoroughly, not to go to sleep in bear-beds at the Zoo.

Anathema also be upon those vandals who demand that bad ogres and witches be met with moral suasion only. Such treatment is lacking in poetic justice, and from the children's standpoint is neither moral nor satisfactory.

There yet remain for consideration a host of modern wonder tales, not belonging to folk-literature. Many of these are grotesquely humorous, in the way children love. Their chief value lies in literary quality or in the fun and joy they give, and also in some ethical teaching. Occasionally, as in a few of Andersen's fairy tales, and in Kennedy's "New World Fairy-Book," there is a slight background of folk-lore on which the author has built original stories, but for the most part the wonder-stories are original productions. Some fine examples of wonder-tales may be found in Andersen's fairy tales, Browne's "Granny's Wonderful Chair," Carroll's "Alice in Wonderland," Madame d'Aulnoy's fairy tales, and Ruskin's "King of the Golden River."

Such, then, is the educational mission of folk-literature and wonder tales; to cultivate the imagination, to prepare for the future understanding of classic literature,—especially poetry,—to develop the sense of beauty, to implant ideas of simple virtues, and last but not least to give joy to children.

J. Berg Esenwein (*Children's Stories and How to Tell Them*):

The commonest form in which the childish imagination finds exercise is that of fairy-tales; but education must take care that it has these in their proper shape as national productions, and that they are not the morbid kind which artificial poetry so often gives us in this species of literature, and which not seldom degenerate into sentimental caricatures and silliness.

—J. K. F. Rosencrantz, *Philosophy of Education.*

The old stories of the race are not fact, but they are truth which the race-mind has visioned and given form in words. They are the product of primitive man's longings and wonderings. They are the answers of his soul in his quest for God. They are his attempts to solve the mystery of his own life, the explanation of his environment. They are the charts which his imagination made, marking the paths by which his spirit might pass to freedom. In them he defied time, conquered space, and transcended all limitations. In them, supernatural agencies were his reserve power. In time of stress, the modern man falls back upon his own sub-conscious self; primitive man called upon the Fairies and kindred beings which his own fancy had created to meet his need.

Thus all such tales embody the ideals of early man, and through them his growth of spirit may be traced. They have even moulded the religious and social life of the present time, for the highest and best achievements of today are but the slow fulfillment of man's age-long prophecies and dreams.

It is because folk and fairy tales are filled with this spirit of truth that they lay hold upon the heart of childhood from generation to generation. As we have said in an earlier chapter, the child, to some extent, repeats the experiences of the race. Light and darkness, wind and sun, sea, sky, and earth surround him. He wonders and dreams about them all. The life within himself calls to the life without and asks Whence? Whither? What? His questionings must find answer on the plane of his own understanding, so the folk tale with its simplicity and sincerity meets his need.

Since belief in the Fairies was a part of primitive man's religion, to feed the child's imagination with the tales which true belief built concerning these supernatural agencies is to awaken in him a religious attitude. The transition is easily made from interest in these representations of the religion and philosophy of our ancestors to a deepened interest in the power of the unseen forces of nature. This belief in an unseen world leads the child directly into the realm of pure spirit. The attitude of wonder is closely akin to reverence.

Fairy tales give the child a sense of well-being. In them good always comes to good; somehow, somewhere, things tend to come out right for the man who chooses wisely and does his best. This attitude of mind is a valuable asset to the child. It adds to his power of endurance and courage, it robs him of fear.

Fairy tales people the child's world, and make him less alone. Fits of intense loneliness frequently sweep over a sensitive child. If he feels the nearness of these unseen friends, his heart is comforted in a way unbelievable to the grown-up who has never known these dream companions. The child who peeps into the cup of every flower for the fairy which may be cradled there will go through life with spirit on tiptoe. Each day will be a new adventure, each road will lead to fortune.

As for myths, they especially need adaptation lest younger children gather wrong ethical ideals from the forms in which the myths come to us, from Greece and Rome particularly. Wise choice must be exercised as to what to omit, what to alter and what to relate unchanged.

Katherine Cather (*Educating by Storytelling*):

When the child leaves the rhythmic, realistic period he enters a world of make-believe and no longer desires tales and jingles that are nothing more than a recounting of facts he already knows. He delights in playing he is some one other than himself, in pretending he is doing things beyond the range of his possibilities, and because he craves a larger experience he craves also fanciful, imaginative tales in which he may have those experiences. He knows that bees sting, that the dog has a cold, wet nose, that the cat lands on its feet, and the squirrel holds its tail up. He wonders about these things, but he is still too limited in experience and in mental capacity to give them real theoretical meaning. Consequently he enjoys the wonder tale, or, as some authorities term it, the "primitive-why story." Early racial tales are those of forest and plain, varying according to the locality in which they originated, from the lion and tiger stories of India and Central Africa to the kangaroo fables of the Australian aborigine.

Primitive man through fear and fancy personified the forces of nature and gave them human attributes, and because they were less tangible than the creatures of jungle and plain that figured in his earliest fables, his mind visioned them as fantastic beings, sometimes lovely and sometimes grotesque, fairies and goblins, destructive monsters and demons, and avenging giants who preserved him from that which he feared. Thus originated the fairy story that was the expression of his religion. The child enjoys these tales.

The narrator can gather this material with comparative ease because the science of ethnology has brought to light many of these tales from primitive literature, and not a few of them have been put into collections available to child workers.

The fairy tale that grew out of the life of the race is also rich in material for children of this period. By "fairy tale" is meant that type of story usually associated with the names of Grimm, Perrault, and Bechstein. Little people delight in it, and will listen to it again and again. Yet because of lack of understanding on the part of parents and teachers, the fairy story often proves to be the rock upon which the child craft meets disaster. Because these tales have had a mighty place in the history of the race and still have their work in the education of the child, it does not follow that they should be fed to young listeners as so much unassorted grain is fed to chickens. There are many that should not be used at all. Those that are used should be carefully graded, because a child will enjoy a narrative in which children are heroes, long before he enjoys one in which adults hold the center of the stage. The father and mother, brothers, sisters, uncles, cousins, and aunts mean much to him because they are part of his experience. But he does not know officers of the state and nation. He does not know lawmakers and magistrates and judges, and tales in which they have a part are less interesting to him than those whose characters are familiar personages. For instance, he is charmed by "Little Red Hen" or "The Three Bears" at an age when "Beauty and the Beast" or "Sleeping Beauty" mean little to him, and a good rule to guide the storyteller in the grading of fairy tales is the well-known pedagogical one, "Proceed from the known to the unknown, from the simple to the complex." Give first those stories whose heroes are familiar personages, then introduce those with characters not so well known.

The mention of fairy tales in education often raises the question, "Is there not danger of making liars of children by feeding them on these stories?" It seems to me the best answer is given by Georg Ebers, the Egyptologist and novelist, in his fascinating autobiography. *The Story of My Life.* Out of his own experience, he handles the subject of fairy tales sincerely and convincingly, and his words are worthy of consideration by every child worker.

"When the time for rising came," he says, "I climbed joyfully into my mother's warm bed, and never did I listen to more beautiful fairy tales than at those hours. They became instinct with life to me and have always remained so. How real became the distress of persecuted innocence, the terrors and charm of the forest, the joys and splendors of the fairy realm! If the flowers in the garden had raised their voices in song, if the birds on the boughs had called and spoken to me, nay, if a tree had changed into a beautiful fairy or the toad in the damp path of our shaded avenue into a witch, it would have been only natural.

"It is a singular thing that actual events which happened in those early days have largely vanished from my memory, but the fairy tales I heard and secretly experienced became firmly impressed on my mind. Education and life provided for my familiarity with reality in all its harshness and angles, its strains and hurts, but who, in those later years, could have flung wide the gates of the kingdom where everything is beautiful and good, and where ugliness is as surely doomed to destruction as evil to punishment? Therefore I plead with voice and pen in behalf of fairy tales. Therefore I give them to my children and grandchildren and have even written a volume of them myself.

"All sensible mothers will doubtless, like ours, take care that the children do not believe the stories which they tell them to be true. I do not remember any time when, if my mind had been called upon to decide, I should have thought anything I invented myself really happened; but I know that we were often unable to distinguish whether the plausible tale invented by some one else belonged to the realm of fact or fiction. On such occasions we appealed to my mother, and her answer instantly set all doubts at rest, for we thought she could never be mistaken and knew that she always told the truth.

"As to the stories I invented myself, I fared like other imaginative children. I could imagine the most marvelous things about every member of the household, and while telling them, but only during that time, I often fancied they were true. Yet the moment I was asked whether these things had actually occurred, it seemed that I woke from a dream. I at once separated what I imagined from what I actually experienced, and it never would have occurred to me to persist against my better knowledge. So the vividly awakened power of imagination led neither me, my brothers and sisters, nor my children and grandchildren into falsehood."

Dr. Ebers' words are based on sound psychology. The child's imaginative nature should be developed, but there should never be any doubt in his mind as to what is make-believe and what is real. Let him wander at will through every realm of fancy, along its sun-kissed highways, among its shadowy glens and wild cascades, but let him realize it is a world of make-believe, not of fact, which he inhabits during that period. His imagination will be as much aroused, his emotional nature will be stirred as deeply, and there will be no discovery later that his mother or teacher deceived him, no temptation to present as fact what he knows to be purely fancy, which is a certain step toward the field of falsehood. If he questions whether a fairy story is true or not, tell him, "No, but once upon a time people thought it was true," and picture how the early tribesmen sat around the fire at night listening to tales told by some of their wise men, just as Indians and Eskimos do to this day. It will make him sympathetic toward the struggles of his remote forefathers, and he will not think the narrator tried to dupe him, nor will he regard the narrative itself as a silly yarn. It will be a dignified tale to him because it was believed in the long ago.

Since we can give only according to the measure in which we possess, whoever tells fairy stories to children ought to know something of their history and meaning. He should have some understanding of how they have come from the depths of the past to their present form, some idea of the work of notable collectors, and some insight into the fundamental principles of the science of folklore.

There are several theories about the origin of these tales, the first and oldest being that they are sun myths and can be traced back to the Vedas, and the exponents of this belief offer many arguments to prove the truth of their contention. The similarity of tales found among people of widely separated regions, they claim, is evidence that they must have come from a common source, "Little Half-Chick," a Spanish folk tale, is found in slightly different dress among the Kabyles of Africa; "Cinderella," in some form or other, is common to every country of Europe and to several oriental lands; while the Teutonic tale of "Brier Rose" and the French of "Sleeping Beauty" are modifications of the same *conte.* Therefore, the orientalists contend, they must have come from a common source and have been modified to suit conditions of life in lands to which they were carried.

Another theory is that all European fairy tales are remnants of the old mythology of the north, the nucleus of the stories having been carried abroad by the Vikings, while still another theory, the most notable advocate of which was the late Andrew Lang, traces fairy tales to the practices and customs of early man and a totemistic belief in man's descent from animals.

Then there are those also who contend that fairy tales are primitive man's philosophy of nature, his explanation of the working of forces he did not understand. The adherents of this theory admit the similarity of tales found among different tribes, but claim that the incidents, which are few, and the characters, who are types, might occur anywhere. In the French story of "Blue Beard" and the Greek tale of "Psyche" curiosity leads to destruction—in the one case of life, in the other of happiness. In the French "Diamonds and Toads," the Teutonic "Snow White and the Seven Dwarfs," and the Bohemian "The Twelve Months," selfishness brings punishment and kindness reward, while the cruel stepmother, the good prince, and the fairy godmother are common to tales of every nation.

But however authorities disagree as to the origin of these stories, they unite in declaring them to be one of the oldest forms of literature. The first collection of fairy tales of which we have any record was published in Venice in 1550 by Straparola, and was a translation of stories from oriental sources. From Italian the book was done into French and, for those early days when books were rare and costly, had a wide circulation. For almost a century this was the only collection of fairy tales in existence. Then, in 1637, a book was published in Naples, *Il Pentamerone,* which Keightley declares is the best collection of fairy tales ever written. The stories were told in the Neapolitan dialect and were drawn from Sicily, Candia, and Italy proper, where Giambattista Basile had gathered them from the people during years of wandering.

About sixty years later, in a magazine published at The Hague, appeared a story, "La Belle au Bois Dormant," by Charles Perrault, which was none other than the tale we know as "Sleeping Beauty." It did not originate with Perrault, but had been told him in childhood by his nurse, who was a peasant from Picardy. A year later seven other stories appeared, "Red Riding Hood," "Blue Beard," "Puss in Boots,"

"The Fairy," "Cinderella," "Riquet o' the Tuft," and "Hop o' My Thumb." They were published under the title, *Contes du Temps Passé avec Moralités,* and signed, "P. Darmancour." Darmancour was a stepson of Perrault, and wrote them at the older man's request from the nurse's tales; so they live in literature as Perrault's work. After this French collector came the German scholars, the Grimms, who gathered and preserved the folklore of Thuringian peasants; Goethe, the Sage of Weimar; Madame Villeneuve; Ruskin; Andrew Lang; and several others. Each of these added to the work begun by Straparola and Basile, until now we have tales from almost every nation, tales proving that a belief in the supernatural is common to primitive people in every clime.

Another aspect wonderfully interesting in the study of fairy tales is the distinctive features of those of different regions, which are so marked that they can be classified according to the locality and topography of the region in which they originated. The largest number of these supernatural beliefs is found among nations whose scenery is wild and rugged, where there are mountains, morasses, dangerous cataracts, and tempestuous oceans, while in flat, cultivated countries away from the sea the fairy superstition is not so strong and the tales are less fantastic. This fact argues powerfully in favor of the Aryan theory that they are primitive man's philosophy of nature, the expression of his religion, and some educators claim that as they were religious stories to the race, they still are religious to the child.

Whether this theory is accepted or refuted, there can be no doubt in the mind of a thinking person that if fairy tales are given to children they should be given intelligently and with discrimination. The narrator should exercise care in their selection, and have some fixed principles to govern that selection, because of the quantity and doubtful literary and ethical quality of much juvenile material.

Many modern fairy stories are not fit to give to children. In selecting fanciful tales for this period of childhood, choose first of all the old ones, those that originated in the childhood of the race, the stories of Grimm, Perrault, and Bechstein. They have stood the test of the ages. They are expressed in beautiful language, they create ideals and arouse inspiration, they feed and satisfy.

There are some fairy tales of later origin that are the works of great writers and deserve the name of literature. First on this list come those of Hans Christian Andersen. "The Three Bears" of Robert Southey is another good example, and sometimes we find floating through magazines and in books of recent issue, fairy tales that are excellent ones to give to children, because they have all the elements of the racial tales. Notable among these is "The Wonder Box" by Will Bradley. But, if there be any doubt in the mind of the narrator about the merit of modern stories, he had better eliminate them from his list and use only those that have stood the test of the ages.

However, even among racial tales the narrator will come upon pitfalls unless judgment mark his selection. The conditions governing his struggle for existence gave primitive man a harsh standard, and consequently his literature is often tinged with a vindictive spirit wholly out of keeping with the ideals of today. Stories in which cruelty, revenge, and bloodshed have a large part should never be told to the young child, no matter what their age or origin. "Blue Beard" is a good example. Although itself a classic, and a recital of the deeds of a French ruler whose name is a synonym of infamy, this tale and all similar tales should be tabooed from the world of little people.

Charles Dickens was the first man in England whose voice carried weight to plead for fairy tales as a part of the school curriculum, and within a few years Dickens found it necessary to oppose the usage of stories that were corrupting the children of the British Isles. Because they were urged to tell fairy tales, unthinking teachers told any that they found, even those in which all the savagery of early man was portrayed. Accounts of beheadings and man-eatings became part of the daily program, and many acts of cruelty among children were traceable to these stories. Instead of teaching forbearance, courtesy, consideration of the poor and aged, and abhorrence of brute force, which the wisely chosen fairy tale will do, story-telling was turning the children into young savages. If the dominant element in a story is cruelty, strike that tale from the list; for even though the deed be punished in the end, the fact that the attention of an unkind child is focused upon cruel acts often leads him to experiment and see what will happen. And I plead also for the elimination from the story-teller's list of every tale in which an unkind or drunken parent plays a part, even though the tale itself be a literary gem. The father or mother is the child's ideal, and it is not the mission of the narrator to shatter that ideal. Even if little folk have discovered that there are delinquent parents in the world, it is a mental shock to have that fact emphasized, and the story that shocks in any way had better be left untold.

Sometimes the elimination or modification of a cruel feature of a tale makes it suitable for telling to children, as in "Hansel and Gretel." The ending Humperdinck uses in his opera, wherein the old witch turns to gingerbread instead of being baked in the oven by the orphans, is far better ethically than the original one, yet the elemental part of the story is left unspoiled. Narrators cannot be too careful in this respect; for the function of story-telling is to refine rather than to brutalize, to give pleasure and not to shock, and there is no excuse for using tales that corrupt or injure in any way when there are enough lovely ones to satisfy every normal desire of the child. Let the test of selection be the question, Does this story contain an element or picture that will shock a sensitive child or whet the cruel tendencies of a rough, revengeful one? If it does, do not use it even though the list of fairy tales may be reduced to a very limited one, but choose the other material for this period from the lore of science that will feed the fancy and not warp the soul or distort the character.

Julia Darrow Cowles (*The Art of Storytelling*):

The child's ability to understand is far in advance of his ability to read, and the old folk-tales which have been handed down orally from generation to generation, and later gathered into volumes for the children of all nations to enjoy together, are a veritable mine of delight to both story-teller and listener.

Folk tales and fairy tales are so interwoven that it is difficult to separate them. That some of both are open to criticism is conceded, but with such abundance of supply there is no need of telling a story which presents even a doubt as to its value.

In her introduction to "The Story Hour," Kate Douglas Wiggin says: "Some universal spiritual truth underlies the really fine old fairy tale; but there can be no educational influence in the so-called fairy stories, which are merely jumbles of impossible incidents, and which not infrequently present dishonesty, deceit, and cruelty in attractive or amusing guise." Here we have the true test which anyone may apply: an underlying "universal spiritual truth." Does our story contain such?

Two very familiar nursery tales which owe their origin to the folk-lore of old—namely, "Jack, the Giant Killer," and "Cinderella"—have recently been brought into question upon the ground of their moral teaching. The critics in question look upon Jack as a thief and a murderer, who "lived happily ever after" upon his ill-gotten gains. For my own part, I find less to condemn in Jack's treatment of the Giant, than in making a hero of a boy who was lazy and disobedient. The Giant had robbed and killed Jack's father, and he was wicked and cruel to all, and Jack could scarcely be blamed for trying to regain his father's stolen wealth, or for cutting down the bean-stalk when the Giant was descending for the purpose of killing him and, in all probability, his mother. But the false note in the story, to my mind, lies in selecting a boy who was avowedly lazy, idle, disobedient, and neglectful of his mother, for the hero of a tale of such marvelous deeds. The tale of Jack, the Giant Killer, however, has many versions, and there is no need whatever, when telling the story, of giving to Jack any of these undesirable traits. Rather, picture him as a boy capable of performing heroic deeds. The change is easily made.

On the other hand, I would champion the story of "Cinderella." The recent criticism brought against this story is that it leads boys and girls to believe that all step-mothers are cruel. I do not think so. The stories of "The Babes in the Woods," and of "The Princes in the Tower," do not teach that all uncles are cruel. Of course the fact that Cinderella's step-mother was a step-mother might be so emphasized in the telling as to give this impression, but it is not emphasized in the story—not, at least, in most of the versions which I have read. Selfishness and pride are set forth in the half-sisters in all their unattractiveness; while Cinderella's final triumph serves as a means of showing her gentle and forgiving nature. These are the points to be brought out in the story-telling, and it would seem to me to be an unjustifiable robbery to take the story of Cinderella from the child's early store of fairy tales. What a thrill of exquisite delight is felt by the child when the magic of the godmother's wand turns Cinderella's rags into the robe of a princess and she is whirled away in her golden chariot to meet the prince. It is a story of goodness rewarded and of evil punished, but all in such a magical and wonderful way! I can feel the early thrill of it yet—and so can you.

There are different versions of both these stories, and it is not a difficult matter to tell either one in such a way as to do away with all objectionable features. As was shown in a previous chapter, much of the impression which a story leaves is due to the manner of its telling. The story of Cinderella certainly contains the "underlying universal, spiritual truth," and so answers to the test of a truly "fine old fairy tale."

American story tellers should not go far afield for their tales of folk lore, and overlook the two distinctive sources afforded by our own country. The stories of the North American Indian, told by camp fire or in tepee, are full of poetic imagery, of symbolic truth, and of heroic valor. They form the original legendary lore of our land, and they should be told to the children, preparing them for a later reading of the poets and authors who have shown us the picturesque as well as the tragic side of the history of the Red Man.

Emelyn Partridge (*Story-telling in School and Home*):

Fairy-Tales include a great number of stories found all over the world; and, strictly speaking, many stories in which the fairy of the conventional type does not appear. In general, the fairy-tale may be said to comprise all those folk-tales dealing with strange or supernatural events, in a mood of half -belief or pure fancy.

There is almost nothing that shows so clearly the difference between the old education and the new as the attitude toward such literature as the fairy-tale. Although in the past, the school may have recognised the fairy-story as a pastime for the child, it certainly scorned all such things in the serious business of education. But now we may almost say that the stone that was rejected has become the head of the corner.

The value of the fairy-tale consists especially in its religious significance. We have seen that it has grown out of religious story. It is still religious for the child, for it is believed. It serves the purpose of stimulating belief in the unseen world. It keeps the supernatural alive and real to the child, shows the world full of friendliness and exalts the good-will principle. It fosters a feeling of safety in the midst of rough forces of nature. In the fairy-tale the child quite unconsciously perceives his own life situation. Fear, imagination, ignorance begin at an early age to make life hard for the child. The world begins to seem alien to him, and he is often lonely in the vastness of it. The fairy-story presents to him a warmth of interest behind nature. In this story his own desires for himself are realised. He sees that out of hard situations good issues for those who are good. It is his compensation for being little and helpless. So we may say that the fairy-tale helps to keep religion alive in the world as almost nothing else does. Behind the pure enjoyment serious forces are at work; and instead of being the most frivolous of fancies, the fairy-tale is one of the most earnest products of the mind of man; and the love of the fairy-story is one of the most significant of the child's interests. It is safe to assert that up to the age of ten the child's taste for these stories may be satisfied to any reasonable extent. Let the child see, through the fairy-story, the play of good and evil in the world. Let him make his judgments upon these deep themes through the medium of his pure enjoyment and his unconscious striving with his own desires. Nothing need be explained to him, and there need be no thought of systematic teaching. The work of the story-teller is simply to satisfy a normal and deep appetite with the best nourishment he can provide. In general, this will be the racial story. There are good folk-tales from almost every land, and these simple stories are far better than the more elaborate and more literary fairy-tales of our own day.

Kate Douglas Wiggin (*The Fairy Ring*):

There was once upon a time a king who had a garden; in that garden was an apple tree, and on that apple tree grew a golden apple every year."

These stories are the golden apples that grew on the tree in the king's garden; grew and grew and grew as the golden years went by; and being apples of gold they could never wither nor shrink nor change, so that they are as beautiful and precious for you to pluck to-day as when first they ripened long, long ago.

Perhaps you do not care for the sort of golden apples that grew in the king's garden; perhaps you prefer plain russets or green pippins? Well, these are not to be despised, for they also are wholesome food for growing boys and girls; but unless you can taste the flavor and feel the magic that lies in the golden apples of the king's garden you will lose one of the joys of youth.

No one can help respecting apples (or stories) that gleam as brightly to-day as they did hundreds and thousands of years ago, when first the tiny blossoms ripened into precious fruit.

> *"Should you ask me whence these stories,*
> *Whence these legends and traditions*
> *With the odors of the forest,*
> *With the dew and damp of meadows?"—*

I can say only that the people were telling fairy tales in Egypt, in Joseph's time, more than three thousand years ago; and that grand old Homer told them in the famous "Odyssey," with its witches and giants, its cap of darkness, and shoes of swiftness. Old nurses and village crones have repeated them by the fireside and in the chimney corner; shepherds and cowherds have recounted them by the brookside, until the children of the world have all learned them by heart, bequeathing them, generation after generation, as a priceless legacy to their own children. Nor must you fancy that they have been told in your own tongue only. Long, long before the art of printing was known, men and women of all nations recited these and similar tales to one another, never thinking that the day would come when they would be regarded as the peculiar property of youth and childhood. There is not a country in Europe, Asia, Africa, Australia, or the islands of the sea where fairy stories of one sort or another have not been current since the dawn of speech; and to make this Fairy Ring of sixty-odd tales the editors have read and sifted as many hundreds. You will miss Cinderella, Red Riding Hood, Jack and the Beanstalk, Toads and Diamonds, Puss in Boots, Bluebeard, Beauty and the Beast, and other favorites, but these have been omitted because they can be easily found in half a dozen volumes already on your shelves, and we preferred to give you in their stead stories less well known and hackneyed.

The so-called Household Tales, such as Drakesbill, The Little Good Mouse, and The Grateful Cobra go back to the times when men thought of animals as their friends and brothers, and in the fireside stories of that period the central figures were often wise and powerful beasts, beasts that had language, assumed human form, and protected as well as served mankind. Frogs, fishes, birds, wolves, cobras, cats, one and all win our sympathy, admiration, and respect as we read of their deeds of prowess, their sagacious counsel, their superhuman power of overcoming obstacles and rescuing from danger or death the golden-haired princess, the unhappy queen mother, or the intrepid but unfortunate prince.

The giants and ogres and witches in the fairy stories need not greatly affright even the youngest readers. For the most part they overreach themselves in ill-doing and are quite at the mercy (as they properly should be) of the brave and virtuous knight or the clever little princess.

If you chance to be an elder brother or sister it may surprise and distress you to find that all the grace, courage, wit, and beauty, as well as most of the good fortune, are vested in the youngest member of the household. The fairy-tale family has customs of its own when it comes to the distribution of vices and virtues, and the elder sons and daughters are likely to be haughty, selfish, and cruel, while the younger ones are as enchantingly beautiful as they are marvelously amiable. The malevolent stepmother still further complicates the domestic situation, and she is so wicked and malicious that if it were not for the dear and delightful one in your own household, or the equally lovable one next door, you might think stepmothers worse than ogres or witches. I cannot account for this prejudice, except that perhaps the ideal of another love and mother goodness has always been so high in the world that the slightest deviation from it has been held up to scorn. As for the superhuman youngest son and daughter, perhaps they are used only to show us that the least and humblest things and persons are capable of becoming the mightiest and most powerful.

Wiseacres (and people who have no love for golden apples) say that in many of these tales "The greater the rogue the better his fortune"; but the Grimm brothers, most famous and most faithful of fairy-tale collectors, reply that the right user of these narratives "will find no evil therein, but, as an old proverb has it, merely a witness of his own heart. Children point at the stars without fear, while others, as the popular superstition goes, thereby offend the angels."

The moment you have plucked a golden apple from the magic tree in the king's garden (which phrase, being interpreted, means whenever you begin one of the tales in this book) you will say farewell to time and space as readily as if you had put on a wishing cap, or a pair of seven league boots, or had blown an elfin pipe to call the fairy host. It matters not when anything happened. It is "Once upon a time," or "A long time ago." As to just where, that is quite as uncertain and unimportant, for we all feel familiar with the fairy-tale landscape, which has delightful features all its own, and easily recognizable. The house is always in the heart of a deep, deep wood like the one "amidst the forest darkly green" where Snowwhite lived with the dwarfs. You know the Well at the World's End whence arose the Frog Prince; the Glass Mountain that Cinderlad climbed, first in his copper, then in his silver, then in his golden armor; the enchanted castle where the White Cat dwelt; the sea over which Faithful John sailed with the Princess of the Golden Roof.

In the story of The Spindle, the Shuttle, and the Needle, the prince has just galloped past the cottage in the wood where the maiden is turning her wheel, when the spindle leaps out of her hand to follow him on his way—leaps and dances and pursues him along the woodland path, the golden thread dragging behind. Then the prince turns (fairy princes always turn at the right time), sees the magic spindle, and, led by the shimmering thread, finds his way back to the lovely princess, the sweetest, loveliest, thriftiest, most bewitching little princess in the whole world, and a princess he might never have found had it not been for the kind offices of the spindle, shuttle, and needle.

This book is the magic spindle; the stories that were golden apples have melted into a golden thread, a train of bright images that will lead you into a radiant country where no one ever grows old; where, when the prince finds and loves the princess, he marries her and they are happy ever after; where the obstacles of life melt under the touch of comprehending kindness; where menacing clouds of misfortune are blown away by gay good will; and where wicked little trolls are invariably defeated by wise simpletons.

We feel that we can do anything when we journey in this enchanting country. Come, then, let us mount and be off; we can ride fast and far, for imagination is the gayest and fleetest of steeds. Let us climb the gilded linden tree and capture the Golden Bird. Let us plunge into the heart of the Briar Wood where the Rose o' the World lies sleeping. Let us break the spell that holds all her court in drowsy slumber, and then, coming out into the sunshine, mount and ride again into the forest. As we pass the Fairy Tree on the edge of the glade we will pluck a Merry Leaf, for this, when tucked away in belt or pouch, will give us a glad heart and a laughing eye all the day long. We shall meet ogres, no doubt, and the more the merrier, for, like Finette, we have but to cry "Abracadabra!" to defeat not ogres only, but wicked bailiffs, stewards, seneschals, witch hags, and even the impossibly vicious stepmother! Cormoran and Blunderbore will quail before us, for our magic weapons, like those of Cornish Jack, will be all-powerful. Then, flushed with triumph we will mount the back of the North Wind and search for the castle that lies East o' the Sun and

West o' the Moon. Daylight will fade, the stars come out, the fire burn low on the hearth, playmates' voices sound unheeded. We shall still sit in the corner of the window seat with the red-covered volume on our knees; for hours ago the magic spindle wrought its spell, and we have been following the golden thread that leads from this work-a-day world into fairyland.

Imagination and Mythology

Kate Douglas Wiggin (*Tales of Wonder*):

There is a Chinese tale, known as "The Singing Prisoner," in which a friendless man is bound hand and foot and thrown into a dungeon, where he lies on the cold stones unfed and untended.

He has no hope of freedom and as complaint will avail him nothing, he begins to while away the hours by reciting poems and stories that he had learned in youth. So happily does he vary the tones of the speakers, feigning in turn the voices of kings and courtiers, lovers and princesses, birds and beasts, that he speedily draws all his fellow-prisoners around him, beguiling them by the spell of his genius.

Those who have food, eagerly press it upon him that his strength may be replenished; the jailer, who has been drawn into the charmed circle, loosens his bonds that he may move more freely, and finally grants him better quarters that the stories may be heard to greater advantage. Next the petty officers hear of the prisoner's marvellous gifts and report them everywhere with such effect that the higher authorities at last become interested and grant him a pardon.

Tales like these, that draw children from play and old men from the chimney-corner; that gain the freedom of a Singing Prisoner, and enable a Scheherazade to postpone from night to night her hour of death, are one and all pervaded by the same eternal magic. Pain, grief, terror, care, and bondage are all forgotten for a time when lakes of gems and enchanted waterfalls shimmer in the sunlight, when Rakshas's palaces rise, full-built, before our very eyes, or when Caballero's Knights of the Fish prance away on their magic chargers. "I wonder when!" "I wonder how!" "I wonder where!" we say as we follow them into the land of mystery. So Youngling said when he heard the sound of the mysterious axe in the forest and asked himself who could be chopping there.

"I wonder!" he cried again when he listened to the faerie spade digging and delving at the top of the rocks.

"I wonder!" he questioned a third time when he drank from the streamlet and sought its source, finding it at last in the enchanted walnut. Axe and spade and walnut each gladly welcomed him, you remember, saying, "It's long I've been looking for you, my lad!" for the new world is always awaiting its Columbus.

No such divine curiosity as that of Youngling's stirred the dull minds of his elder brothers and to them came no such reward. They jeered at the wanderer, reproaching him that he forever strayed from the beaten path, but when Youngling issues from the forest with the magic axe, the marvellous spade, and the miraculous nut to conquer his little world, we begin to ask ourselves which of the roads in the wood are indeed best worth following.

"Childish wonder is the first step in human wisdom," said the greatest of the world's showmen, but there are no wonders to the eyes that lack real vision. In the story of "What the Birds Said," for instance, the stolid jailer flatly denies that the feathered creatures have any message of import to convey; it is the poor captive who by sympathy and insight divines the meaning of their chatter and thus saves the city and his own life.

The tales in this book are of many kinds of wonder; of black magic, white magic and gray; ranging from the recital of strange and supernatural deeds and experiences to those that foreshadow modern conquests of nature and those that utilize the marvellous to teach a moral lesson. Choose among them as you will, for as the Spaniards might say, "The book is at your feet; whatever you admire is yours!"

"Tales of Wonder" is the fourth and last of our Fairy Series in the Children's Classics, so this preface is in the nature of an epilogue. "The Fairy Ring," "Magic Casements," "Tales of Laughter" each had its separate message for its little public, and "Tales of Wonder" rings down the curtain.

There was once a little brown nightingale that sang melodious strains in the river-thickets of the Emperor's garden, but when she was transported to the Porcelain Palace the courtiers soon tired of her wild-wood notes and supplanted her with a wonderful bird-automaton, fashioned of gold and jewels.

Time went on, but the Emperor, wisest of the court, began at last to languish, and to long unceasingly for the fresh, free note of the little brown nightingale. It was sweeter by far than the machine-made trills and roulades of the artificial songster, and he felt instinctively that only by its return could death be charmed away.

The old, yet ever new, tales in these four books are like the wild notes of the nightingale in the river-thicket, and many are the emperors to whom they have sung.

Whenever we tire of what is trivial and paltry in the machine-made fairy tale of to-day, let us open one of these crimson volumes and hear again the note of the little brown bird in the thicket.

Charles Kingsley (*The Heroes*):

My dear Children,

Some of you have heard already of the old Greeks; and all of you, as you grow up, will hear more and more of them. Those of you who are boys will, perhaps, spend a great deal of time in reading Greek books; and the girls, though they may not learn Greek, will be sure to come across a great many stories taken from Greek history, and to see, I may say every day, things which we should not have had if it had not been for these old Greeks. You can hardly find a well-written book which has not in it Greek names, and words, and proverbs; you cannot walk through a great town without passing Greek buildings; you cannot go into a well-furnished room without seeing Greek statues and ornaments, even Greek patterns of furniture and paper; so strangely have these old Greeks left their mark behind them upon this modern world in which we now live. And as you grow up, and read more and more, you will find that we owe to these old Greeks the beginnings of all our mathematics and geometry—that is, the science and knowledge of numbers, and of the shapes of things, and of the forces which make things move and stand at rest; and the beginnings of our geography and astronomy; and of our laws, and freedom, and politics—that is, the science of how to rule a country, and make it peaceful and strong. And we owe to them, too, the beginning of our logic—that is, the study of words and of reasoning; and of our metaphysics—that is, the study of our own thoughts and souls. And last of all, they made their language so beautiful that foreigners used to take to it instead of their own; and at last Greek became the common language of educated people all over the old world, from Persia and Egypt even to Spain and Britain. And therefore it was that the New Testament was written in Greek, that it might be read and understood by all the nations of the Roman empire; so that, next to the Jews, and the Bible which the Jews handed down to us, we owe more to these old Greeks than to any people upon earth.

Now you must remember one thing—that 'Greeks' was not their real name. They called themselves always 'Hellens,' but the Romans miscalled them Greeks; and we have taken that wrong name from the Romans—it would take a long time to tell you why. They were made up of many tribes and many small separate states; and when you hear in this book of Minuai, and Athenians, and other such names, you must remember that they were all different tribes and peoples of the one great Hellen race, who lived in what we now call Greece, in the islands of the Archipelago, and along the coast of Asia Minor-Ionia, as they call it—from the Hellespont to Rhodes, and had afterwards colonies and cities in Sicily, and South Italy—which was called Great

Greece—and along the shores of the Black Sea, at Sinope, and Kertch, and at Sevastopol. And after that, again, they spread under Alexander the Great, and conquered Egypt, and Syria, and Persia, and the whole East. But that was many hundred years after my stories; for then there were no Greeks on the Black Sea shores, nor in Sicily, or Italy, or anywhere but in Greece and in Ionia. And if you are puzzled by the names of places in this book, you must take the maps and find them out. It will be a pleasanter way of learning geography than out of a dull lesson-book.

Now, I love these old Hellens heartily; and I should be very ungrateful to them if I did not, considering all that they have taught me; and they seem to me like brothers, though they have all been dead and gone many hundred years ago. So as you must learn about them, whether you choose or not, I wish to be the first to introduce you to them, and to say, 'Come hither, children, at this blessed Christmas time, when all God's creatures should rejoice together, and bless Him who redeemed them all. Come and see old friends of mine, whom I knew long ere you were born. They are come to visit us at Christmas, out of the world where all live to God; and to tell you some of their old fairy tales, which they loved when they were young like you.'

For nations begin at first by being children like you, though they are made up of grown men. They are children at first like you—men and women with children's hearts; frank, and affectionate, and full of trust, and teachable, and loving to see and learn all the wonders round them; and greedy also, too often, and passionate and silly, as children are.

Thus these old Greeks were teachable, and learnt from all the nations round. From the Phœnicians they learnt shipbuilding, and some say letters beside; and from the Assyrians they learnt painting, and carving, and building in wood and stone; and from the Egyptians they learnt astronomy, and many things which you would not understand. In this they were like our own forefathers the Northmen, of whom you love to hear, who, though they were wild and rough themselves, were humble, and glad to learn from every one. Therefore God rewarded these Greeks, as He rewarded our forefathers, and made them wiser than the people who taught them in everything they learnt; for He loves to see men and children open-hearted, and willing to be taught; and to him who uses what he has got, He gives more and more day by day. So these Greeks grew wise and powerful, and wrote poems which will live till the world's end, which you must read for yourselves some day, in English at least, if not in Greek. And they learnt to carve statues, and build temples, which are still among the wonders of the world; and many another wondrous thing God taught them, for which we are the wiser this day.

For you must not fancy, children, that because these old Greeks were heathens, therefore God did not care for them, and taught them nothing.

The Bible tells us that it was not so, but that God's mercy is over all His works, and that He understands the hearts of all people, and fashions all their works. And St. Paul told these old Greeks in after times, when they had grown wicked and fallen low, that they ought to have known better, because they were God's offspring, as their own poets had said; and that the good God had put them where they were, to seek the Lord, and feel after Him, and find Him, though He was not far from any one of them. And Clement of Alexandria, a great Father of the Church, who was as wise as he was good, said that God had sent down

Philosophy to the Greeks from heaven, as He sent down the Gospel to the Jews.

For Jesus Christ, remember, is the Light who lights every man who comes into the world. And no one can think a right thought, or feel a right feeling, or understand the real truth of anything in earth and heaven, unless the good Lord Jesus teaches him by His Spirit, which gives man understanding.

But these Greeks, as St. Paul told them, forgot what God had taught them, and, though they were God's offspring, worshipped idols of wood and stone, and fell at last into sin and shame, and then, of course, into cowardice and slavery, till they perished out of that beautiful land which God had given them for so many years.

For, like all nations who have left anything behind them, beside mere mounds of earth, they believed at first in the One True God who made all heaven and earth. But after a while, like all other nations, they began to worship other gods, or rather angels and spirits, who—so they fancied—lived about their land. Zeus, the Father of gods and men—who was some dim remembrance of the blessed true God—and

Hera his wife, and Phœbus Apollo the Sun-god, and Pallas Athene who taught men wisdom and useful arts, and Aphrodite the Queen of Beauty, and Poseidon the Ruler of the Sea, and Hephaistos the King of the Fire, who taught men to work in metals. And they honoured the Gods of the Rivers, and the Nymph-maids, who they fancied lived in the caves, and the fountains, and the glens of the forest, and all beautiful wild places. And they honoured the Erinnues, the dreadful sisters, who, they thought, haunted guilty men until their sins were purged away. And many other dreams they had, which parted the One God into many; and they said, too, that these gods did things which would be a shame and sin for any man to do. And when their philosophers arose, and told them that God was One, they would not listen, but loved their idols, and their wicked idol feasts, till they all came to ruin. But we will talk of such sad things no more.

But, at the time of which this little book speaks, they had not fallen as low as that. They worshipped no idols, as far as I can find; and they still believed in the last six of the ten commandments, and knew well what was right and what was wrong. And they believed—

and that was what gave them courage—that the gods loved men, and taught them, and that without the gods men were sure to come to ruin. And in that they were right enough, as we know—more right even than they thought; for without God we can do nothing, and all wisdom comes from Him.

Now, you must not think of them in this book as learned men, living in great cities, such as they were afterwards, when they wrought all their beautiful works, but as country people, living in farms and walled villages, in a simple, hard-working way; so that the greatest kings and heroes cooked their own meals, and thought it no shame, and made their own ships and weapons, and fed and harnessed their own horses; and the queens worked with their maid-servants, and did all the business of the house, and spun, and wove, and embroidered, and made their husbands' clothes and their own. So that a man was honoured among them, not because he happened to be rich, but according to his skill, and his strength, and courage, and the number of things which he could do. For they were but grown-up children, though they were right noble children too; and it was with them as it is now at school—the strongest and cleverest boy, though he be poor, leads all the rest.

Now, while they were young and simple they loved fairy tales, as you do now. All nations do so when they are young: our old forefathers did, and called their stories 'Sagas.' I will read you some of them some day—some of the Eddas, and the Voluspa, and Beowulf, and the noble old Romances. The old Arabs, again, had their tales, which we now call the 'Arabian Nights.' The old Romans had theirs, and they called them 'Fabulæ,' from which our word 'fable' comes; but the old Hellens called theirs 'Muthoi,' from which our new word 'myth' is taken. But next to those old Romances, which were written in the Christian middle age, there are no fairy tales like these old Greek ones, for beauty, and wisdom, and truth, and for making children love noble deeds, and trust in God to help them through.

Now, why have I called this book 'The Heroes'? Because that was the name which the Hellens gave to men who were brave and skilful, and dare do more than other men. At first, I think, that was all it meant: but after a time it came to mean something more; it came to mean men who helped their country; men in those old times, when the country was half-wild, who killed fierce beasts and evil men, and drained swamps, and founded towns, and therefore after they were dead, were honoured, because they had left their country better than they found it. And we call such a man a hero in English to this day, and call it a 'heroic' thing to suffer pain and grief, that we may do good to our fellow-men. We may all do that, my children, boys and girls alike; and we ought to do it, for it is easier now than ever, and safer, and the path more clear. But you shall hear how the Hellens said their heroes worked, three thousand years ago. The stories are not all true, of course, nor half of them; you are not simple enough to fancy that; but the meaning of them is true, and true for ever, and that is—'Do right, and God will help you.'

Mary Helen Beckwith *(In Myth-land):*

My dear little friends:—

A great many, many years ago, more years ago than you can count, there were some people living in a country called Greece that I think you will like to hear about.

They were wise for those times, and knew how to make many beautiful things, but they did not know much about the

> *"Great, wide, beautiful, wonderful world,*
> *With the beautiful water around it curled,"*

nor much about the little country in which they lived; and they had many queer ideas.

"Who takes care of all the things in the world?" they wondered. "One person could not do it, there must be a great many," they thought. When a little boy asked his papa about it, the papa would say, "My child, there are many gods living on Mount Olympus, that high mountain you can see in the east. See, its top touches the blue sky. The gods have beautiful houses built of all manner of precious stones. They give us the things we need, fruit and grain for food, the beautiful flowers, the fish in the sea, the birds of the air, and the wild beasts in the forest. We must be kind and loving, my boy, like the dear gods."

Then perhaps he would tell his little boy of Jupiter, the king in that fair land among the clouds, and of Juno, the queen; of Minerva, the goddess of wisdom; and of Venus, the goddess of beauty.

He would not forget dear little Cupid, who could shoot love into people's hearts with his bow and arrows, nor Mercury, who taught people to be skilful, brave and true. Oh, how swiftly he could run, for he had wings on his shoes. He wore wings on his cap, too; and he sometimes carried a queer staff in his hand.

There were, oh, so many more gods! Apollo, who drove the sun chariot; Diana, who took care of the moon; Ceres, who taught the grain to grow; Peneus, who looked after the brooks and rivers; and Neptune, the god of the sea.

These were not all; but if you want to know about any more ask your mamma or your teacher to tell you of them, and when you go into an Art Gallery look for paintings and statues of them.

A little Greek boy could have told you many things, could he not? "But," I think I hear you say, "we know that there is just one dear Father, who takes care of the things and the people He has made."

Yes, and that is a more beautiful story than any the Greek boy could have told you; but some of his stories are pretty ones, and perhaps you will like to read them.

They have been saved for us all these years; and here are a few that I have told over and over to many little boys and girls, who have enjoyed them very much. I hope you will like them, too.

Sincerely your friend,
M. Helen Beckwith.

Emma Firth (*Stories of Old Greece*):

"There is an instinct in the human heart
Which makes all fables it has coined—
To justify the reign of its belief,
And strengthen it by beauty's right divine—
Veil in their inner cells a mystic gift,
Which, like the hazel twig in faithful hands,
Points surely to the hidden springs of truth."

Aside from their use as a means of strengthening the imagination, the myths embody ethical truths, which are helpful just in proportion to the intellectual activity which the stories arouse. The child lover will seek for the best means in accomplishing her end,—the harmonious culture of the child. In all that she does, she will be governed by the purest motives.

The telling of a story has a broader meaning than that of entertainment. Its real motive is the making of what the child loves a means by which he may be led to a clearer understanding of his own powers and possibilities, and of his relations to others.

The child lives wholly in the present. He is semi-barbaric in his tendencies toward self-interest. He needs to be lifted from an indefinite present of childish pleasure to a definite understanding of his own powers, and a better exercise of his will. If by means of a story, well told, he can grasp the simple truth contained in it, he is making progress in the right direction. He is getting a foundation for the future study of literature, and gaining an appreciation for the beautiful in art.

All modern tendencies are to make children too realistic, and to stifle, rather than to cultivate, the fine imagination necessary to the creation or enjoyment of art and literature. By presenting these myths, the product of a primitive people, and therefore adapted to the child, because of their beauty and simplicity, we are giving him good material for the growth of a healthful imagination.

While the general motive for telling stories is this, there are special motives in each story, which, if thoroughly appreciated, may enhance the value of the story. The first myth, a flower and sun myth, is designed to inspire in the child a feeling for the beauty and dignity of friendship. The story of Phaethon emphasizes the folly of unreasonable requests. Baucis and Philemon teach respect for the aged, and hospitality. The Rhoecus urges the doing of the "duty which lies nearest." In nearly all the myths courage and self-forgetfulness are shown; and by arousing admiration for these qualities we may inspire in the child a desire to possess them.

These myths are meant to do for the little beginner what the study of literature does for the "children of a larger growth." They are but beginnings for beginners; but with the sincere hope that they may accomplish the desired results, the writer submits them to her fellow-teachers and to the dear children of America.

Edward St. John (*Stories and Storytelling*):

The stories which we may use for purposes of moral and religious education may be grouped in two great classes, with several subdivisions under each. These classes may be distinguished as the idealistic and the realistic stories. The first group includes those that are recognized as imaginary in origin or which take liberties with facts, but which embody and set forth principles or truths; the second is made up of those that are or profess to be strictly conformed to fact. The two kinds of stories make their impressions upon the moral nature in somewhat different ways, and that they may be most helpful the distinction between them must be kept clearly in mind by the teacher and certain points must be guarded in the use of each.

Because they are untrue to fact many of the first group are often considered unsuitable for use by the teacher of morals, but a very little thoughtful consideration will show that they have great moral value, and that a large part of their special power is due to this very characteristic. The departure from prosaic and temporary fact is that the ideal and eternal truth may be more strongly emphasized. Events are related that could not possibly have happened, but it does not follow that the tale must have a vicious influence.

Among the important forms of idealistic stories are fairy- and folk-tales, myths, legends, fables, and allegories. Most of these have a moral content, and indeed a moral aim was usually responsible for their origin. The others should be discarded by the teacher of morals, or should be carefully edited with the moral aim in mind.

Most fairy-tales and folk-tales, whether they are modern in origin or, as is true with most of the children's favorites, have come down to us from a very distant past, have this distinctly moral quality, which appears in the fact that virtue is rewarded and wrong-doing receives its punishment. This, the critic will object, is true of real life as well. So much may be granted, but we must remember that "the mills of God grind slowly," and that frequently the child is unable to trace the relation between cause and effect in such cases.

Nature's penalties are sure, but often one must wait a lifetime to see their completion, while sometimes it is upon the next generation that they fall most heavily. When the retribution falls it is often of a kind that the child or untutored adult cannot appreciate in advance.

In fairy-land, on the other hand, penalty quickly, follows offense, and is of a kind that strongly appeals to the motives that influence a child. Hence oftentimes a fairy-tale points a moral more effectively than a story drawn from real life. If there is a valid principle back of the lesson taught there is no danger of moral loss when the child reaches the critical age, unless the story has been presented as one of the realistic type. Children find as much pleasure in stories which they know are the product of another's fancy as they do in playthings which by the power of their own imagination they transform into something very different from what they are.

A myth is in its origin an idea which has been clothed with a poetic garb of fiction. While it is an interpretation of some phenomenon of nature, it is an explanation in terms of human motives and hence has a moral content. It is an attempt at scientific explanation by those who are so unsophisticated as to attribute anthropomorphic personality and motives to all objects about them, which means that it is really a search for principles underlying human conduct. In this sphere the judgments passed are usually true and of real importance.

There is a peculiar charm about the classic myths that gives them special teaching power. This is largely due to the fact that they appeal to those elemental feelings which are common to all men, and which have the dominant place in the lives of primitive races and of children. There is also a special picturesqueness and charm of form which they owe to the fact that they were long preserved in oral form before they were committed to writing. Handed down for many centuries by word of mouth, filtered through the minds of scores of generations, they have been subjected to a continual process of testing and elimination of elements that do not appeal to interest and conform to popular ethical standards until a certain measure of perfection of form and content has been attained.

So great is the charm of the Greek myths, for example, and so strongly do they appeal to the interests of children and youth, that it is with real regret that many teachers have put them aside because of the moral imperfections of the gods and the polytheistic conceptions with which they are filled. They are right in putting the moral and religious results above all others that are involved, and, from the days of Plato on, many educators have felt the same necessity and have reached the same conclusion. But the rejection of all these stories is not as essential as it seems at first thought. The elimination of such of the stories as cannot be so edited as to remove accounts of the grosser forms of immorality and to emphasize the fact that vice and virtue meet their certain rewards meets the ethical requirement. The gods of the Greeks were only men of superhuman powers, and the stories of their lives have the same educational values as others of the ideal type.

The polytheistic element still remains as an objection on the side of religious education, but it may be readily overcome. One may introduce the myth by saying, "You know, children, that our Father in heaven made the earth and everything about us, and that he takes care of us all. Many years ago there were people who had never heard of this; but when they looked out upon the beautiful world and saw the sun rising every morning, and the stars shining at night, and the flowers blooming, and the fruits ripening in the trees, they knew that some one must care for all of these. Since they did not know of the one great God who can do all things they thought that there must be one god for the sun and one for the stars, another for the flowers and still another for the fruits. I am going to tell you of some of the things that they thought these gods did." When one has finished the story he may add, "That is the way they told it long ago, but we know that it is really our Father in heaven who cares for all the creatures that he has made." So the thought of those old days may stir the simple religious feelings of the child—the wonder and love and dread and trust that he shares with the men of that early age—and that without giving him wrong conceptions of God.

Julia Darrow Cowles (*The Art of Storytelling*):

The world is a wonder-palace to the child. "Everything hints at something more magical and more marvelous which is to come." The inanimate objects about him are given living attributes; animals and flowers are endowed by his fancy with human thought and feeling. He talks to the clouds and the stars; he peoples the sky with living inhabitants; to him the winds are not "forces of nature"; they are boisterous companions or gentle friends.

This applies to the imaginative child, and there are more imaginative children than the most of us suspect. The imagination may be suppressed by older and "wiser" companions, or natural shyness may cause the imaginative fancies to remain unvoiced; but the fancies are there—bubbling over in fantastic follies or childish imagery, or kept in those hidden chambers of the soul to which grown-ups are forbidden entrance.

Because of this mental attitude, children are inherent myth-makers. And to the same mental attitude upon the part of the children of the race, is due the fund of mythological lore which has enriched the world's literature and inspired much of its art.

To this rich store, then, the child may be introduced by means of mythological stories. Their appeal is strong because they are in harmony with his own spontaneous interests. Froebel says: "Would'st thou know how to teach the child? Observe him, and he will show you what to do." If, then, the child so loves the myth, let us hold him and help him by means of the mythological story. Those which contain an objectionable element may readily be withheld; there are plenty which are beautiful in their form and true in their teaching.

The myth, strictly speaking, differs from the fairy story in that it personifies the forces and manifestations of nature: Aurora awakening the sleeping world with her shafts of light; Ceres presiding over the harvests of golden grain; Jove hurling the dreadful thunderbolts; and Narcissus living in the beautiful blossom which bears his name.

Few children will accept these stories as absolute statements of fact, nor need they be so presented. Whatever this personification of the universal elements may have meant to the ancient Greeks, to us it is purely imaginary; it is the fairy-land of nature. Children love to "make believe," and their own personifications of the forces of nature, while spontaneous and vivid, are a part of their imaginative world—a part of their "make believe." So, mythological stories are never accepted by them upon the literal plane of the true nature story, nor should they ever be so presented. When stories of the ancient gods and goddesses are told, they may be very briefly outlined as the imaginative stories of an ancient race. This will give them their true place, without in the least detracting from their charm.

The child who is made familiar with the old mythology by means of stories and verse, holds the key of understanding to the countless allusions of the world's best literature. He may not comprehend the deeper meaning, nor understand that they were the religion of an ancient people, but when in his later reading of some masterpiece of poetry or prose he finds an allusion to Phaeton, to Apollo, or to Neptune, he will experience the same delight that comes to one who meets an old playfellow in a foreign land.

Gladys Davidson (*Wonder Tales*):

The religion of the early Greeks and Romans, like that of most of the ancient nations of their time, was very closely interwoven with the history of their country and the deeds of their most famous heroes; and though, before the introduction of Christianity, it had fallen into a very corrupt state, in its earlier and purer forms it had much that was beautiful in it, and many great truths were hidden in the myths and fables relating to the various gods and goddesses worshipped by its adherents.

What we may regard as the foolish pagan practice of worshipping many different gods and goddesses may not have been so entirely foolish from the standpoint of primitive peoples. Those who have made special study of such matters give various explanations as to how the practice may have arisen. The foremost nations of ancient times all had a belief in the existence of gods and goddesses the Babylonians, Assyrians, Egyptians, as well as the Greeks and Romans and the people of ancient India. Naturally, such gods and goddesses are regarded as having each different powers and a different character, and some of them may be looked upon as far more powerful and benevolent than others. Writers tell us that among the Greeks, as among the other ancient peoples, many people were fully convinced that there was one great and splendid God, who was mightier and far above all the others, who were inferior to himself in power and over whom he ruled as a glorious king. This king, or father of the gods, was called by the Greeks Zeus, and by the Romans Jupiter, being familiar to us also by the name Jove.

The more enlightened of the Greeks felt that this mighty God, the lord of the whole universe, must be possessed of every great and good quality they most admired; and since they so highly reverenced these qualities and virtues in him, and he was the head of all, they often spoke as if he were the one and only deity.

Among the other great deities or gods, was Minerva—called Pallas Athene by the Greeks—the Goddess of Wisdom. Two deities strong and mighty in battle were Mars—called Ares by the Greeks—the God of War, and Bellona, his sister, Goddess of Battles. They also worshipped beauty, itself—called Aphrodite by the Greeks, Venus by the Romans—the Goddess of Beauty. Another famous deity was Mercury—called Hermes by the Greeks—the God of cunning, liveliness, and commercial ability. Artistic gifts, again, were represented by Apollo, the God of Music and the Arts, while Cupid—called Eros by the Greeks—was the God of Love.

The marvels of the world of nature were treated and worshipped as deities also—the sun as Apollo, or Phœbus, the sun-god; the moon as the goddess Luna; fire as the god Vulcan; the corn as Ceres; the flowers as Flora; the fruits as Pomona, &c.

Possibly wise men and teachers may have invented some of these gods with the desire that mankind should not forget to render due worship to the powers and goodness of the One Great God and All-Father, nor to be thankful for the wonders He had made and His care for their welfare; and some myths in which these gods and goddesses figure are probably intended, if read aright, to be taken as parables or allegories setting forth some great truth or moral lesson.

Several of these myths and stories are very similar to certain of the stories contained in our Bible and in the great books of other ancient religions; and this is the reason why some students have thought that all religions can be traced to one origin.

However that may be, though the comparison of these myths with the Bible narratives is very interesting and fascinating, I do not propose to go into the subject in this book, but merely to tell you some of the wonderful stories contained in the Greek and Roman fables, so that you may be encouraged to take up the study of these myths and their hidden meanings for yourselves later on.

Most of our knowledge of these myths has been gathered from the beautiful poetry of the ancient Greeks and Romans, and from the wonderful plays written by their greatest writers.

From these authors we learn that the chief home of the gods was believed to be Mount Olympus, a range of high mountains on the boundary of Macedonia and Thessaly; and here the mighty Jupiter reigned as king of the heavens, with his queen, Juno, the glorious Goddess of Marriage, and attended by a court of other gods and goddesses.

The seas were ruled by Neptune, the King-God of the Ocean; and the Under-World, or Land of Shades, where the ancients believed that the spirits of men and women dwelt after death, was ruled by the dreaded god Pluto, the King of Darkness.

All these ruling gods were attended by lesser gods; and they did not always remain in their own abodes, but spent much of their time in visiting the earth, where they often made use of mortals, giants, dwarfs, and even wild beasts in order to carry out their plans.

They were all gifted with magic powers, and some of them could take on the form of any creature they pleased; and though they were often glorious to look upon, they were not always kind or virtuous, and in many of the stories told of them by the ancient writers they are represented as doing cruel deeds.

There are also mentioned in these tales other beings known as nymphs, who were, in reality, lesser goddesses, but who, though of a higher order than ordinary mortal maidens, did not possess the magic powers of the great goddesses; and these fairy-like creatures dwelt in the seas, springs, rivers, grottoes, trees, and mountains. The sea-nymphs were called Oceanides and Nereids; those who dwelt in fresh water, rivers, lakes, brooks, or springs were known as Naiads; the nymphs of the mountains and grottoes were the Oreades; the nymphs of the glens were Napææ; the nymphs of the trees were called Dryads—those who dwelt in oak trees only being known as Hamadryads.

The nymphs were very fair to look upon; and many of them were married to mortals, and some of them to gods.

Besides the nymphs, there were some strange male beings called Satyrs. These were lesser gods of the woods, and were ugly creatures, more like apes than men, but with the cloven feet and horns of goats; and they were wild and noisy in their ways and took great delight in frightening the nymphs and any mortal maidens who came near them.

Many of the stories told of the gods and heroes of the ancient Greeks and Romans are full of wonder and beauty; and in this book I have related some of the most interesting of these tales, in the hope that you may be led thus to read them later on in their original form in the beautiful poetry of these two great nations of the past whose scholars, poets, dramatists, philosophers, mathematicians and sculptors are numbered amongst the greatest the world has ever known.

Grace Kupfer (*Stories of Long Ago*):

Almost all boys and girls like fairy tales; they appeal to the imaginative side of the child's nature. We cannot make school reading effective as a means of education unless we make it a pleasure as well: we must recognize the activity of the imagination in childhood.

Myths are closely akin to fairy tales, and nothing in the whole field of literature can so well serve our purpose. The myths of the Greeks and Romans are especially valuable because they have become an inseparable part of art and literature. They have a historical value, too, in conveying to the reader some idea of the thoughts and habits of the beauty-loving people with whom they originated.

James Wood (*Stories from Greek Mythology*):

The following Tales, composed principally to interest the youthful Reader in the Greek Mythology, are derived partly from the classical originals, and partly from excellent versions of them in German. They are written from a sincere affection for them as fantasies, and a conviction that they contain a high and noble, as well as true meaning,—true, at once, to the spirit and life-theorem of the people among whom they were conceived, and as poetic representations of vital elements in the mystery of life to this hour. The construction they put upon things is a wonderfully just and wise one, and bespeaks high inspirations,—as, indeed, all genuine insight into reality everywhere especially does. The Wisest is omnipresent, and reveals his secrets universally to the seeing eye and the hearing ear. The revelation in all its fulness is nowhere wanting, only the sense to discern it, and the courage to be true to it. The Greeks had natures endowed with intellect and daring of the first quality, lived in manifold fearless just relation to the God's fact, and knew thereby not a little of true wisdom. Their power of fantasy and gift of articulate speech, too, the world has nowhere else seen surpassed or equalled; and the fancies they, with their fine faculties, conceived and cherished were, in no respect, empty, or idle, ones, but earnest withal. They strove to make them images of reality, and, indeed, took pleasure in them, and gained acceptance for them, only as real representations. Not so earnest by any means as the Jews, who stood in awe of the fact far too seriously to attempt fantasies of it. Yet the Greek fancies did reflect and reveal reality with a depth and subtlety of insight, genuineness of sympathy, breadth of conception, and truth of representation, which we in vain seek for in the genius of any other people. Reality is, no doubt, greater, and more vital to know in so real a world and life, than any fiction; and the thoughts of God, which the facts are, are infinitely more precious than the fancies of man about them, or even according to them; yet, is man's power of fancying, or fantasying, in harmony with the fact, the measure of his knowledge of it and vital relationship to it, and the divinely-appointed means withal whereby the fact itself is brought home to our affections. The thoughts of men true to the divine are the key to the thoughts of God; and here, in the Greek Myths especially, we have the Greek fancy, not an unfaithful one, of the God's fact. Read candidly, they speak worthily and truly. Though the properly Christian element, even as an idea, still more as a spirit, is by all accounts absent, there is much in them calculated at once to purify and elevate both the intellect and the heart of the very best among us.

Imagination and the Arabian Nights

Martha Lane (*The Arabian Nights*):

More than two hundred years ago a certain Frenchman, Antoine Galland, who had been connected with the French embassy at Constantinople, began to translate into his own language a series of Arabic tales which had come to his knowledge during his stay in the East. At first the stories were supposed to be for children only, but before long all classes of readers were eagerly awaiting the appearance of the next set of tales. Groups of young men would gather at night beneath Galland's window and call to him, "O you who can tell such wonderful stories, give us just one more!"

As soon as the stories were translated into English, inquiries were made as to the originals. It was discovered that while M. Galland had severely abbreviated the Arabic text he had also inserted narratives of the same kind from other sources to fill the gaps in his collection. Critics agree that he had a discriminating judgment as to what would be most entertaining to European readers, and time has justified his inclusion of what are now known as the "interpolated tales," among which are "Prince Zeyn," "Aladdin," "Ali Baba," "The Talking Bird," "Ali Cogia," and "Prince Ahmed" of this collection. In fact, many of us, if asked to name the most famous of the stories, would mention these before others of undoubted authenticity.

No one knows who wrote the Arabian Nights or when the stories were first collected. Probably they are by many authors and were repeated about Bedouin camp fires or told by professional story-tellers in kings' palaces long before they were put into written form. The caliph Haroun al-Raschid, his wife Zobeide, his vizier Jaafar, and his executioner Mesrour are frequently mentioned in the tales, and as Haroun was a contemporary of Charlemagne, we cannot give to these stories an earlier date than the ninth century. At that period, when most of the Western world was still in the darkness of barbarism and ignorance, and when many European kings could neither read nor write, the Arabians possessed both learning and culture. It is probable that most of the stories were written before the fourteenth century, as in the whole collection there are only three references to coffee-drinking, a custom now so general in the East that its omission in the detailed accounts of feasting and merrymaking is noticeable. Coffee-drinking became common in the fourteenth century, and therefore we must conclude that the stories were not of a later origin.

The Thousand and One Nights, as the collection is sometimes called, makes constant reference to the customs and religious beliefs of the followers of Mohammed. A brief explanation of their faith may not be out of place. They believe in one God, to whom they give the name of Allah, and they have taken several articles of their creed from the Jews and the Christians as well as from the Arabians and Persians. From the Persians came the belief in the existence of genii, or jinn—spirits created of fire, who have strange and magical powers. The Mohammedans are firm believers in the doctrine that all things are planned from the beginning of the world, and that no one can escape the fate that is marked out for him.

The sacred book of the Mohammedans is the Koran, in which they are taught that Allah has revealed himself to various prophets. The Pentateuch, or the first five books of our Bible, the Psalms, and the

Gospels are all regarded by them as holy, but Mohammed is considered the latest and most divine of the prophets. His followers believe in prayer, in morality of life, in fasting and giving alms, and in the pilgrimage to their sacred city of Mecca as an act of worship. They are a temperate and cleanly people, the use of wine being strictly forbidden, and frequent ablutions being required as a religious duty. The devout Mussulman is an exemplary and law-abiding person, honest and kind and helpful in his daily living.

It must be understood, however, that these stories are pure narrative and have no moral or religious significance. They are simply stories, and while they throw interesting side lights on the customs of the time, they were never intended to be instructive. They have become so famous that no one could be considered well-read who failed to recognize a reference to Ali Baba, Sindbad's Voyages, Aladdin's Lamp, or the Enchanted Horse, and therefore they must be included in any course of literary study; but the joy of the reading should be sufficient inducement for all story-lovers.

In the East the collection is known as *Alif laila walaila,* or "A thousand nights and one night." As the study of the ancient texts progressed, many different copies were found. Some of them had been abridged, and it was hard to find two that were alike. It was evident also that each province had added stories which were popular in that particular region. This fact may account in some measure for the many liberties that have been taken in the English editions. Among the latter the most famous are the translations of Jonathan Scott, Sir Richard Burton, Edward William Lane, and John Payne. Dr. Scott made no attempt to furnish a literal translation or to give an oriental flavor to his style; he did precisely what Galland had done in French—that is, he told the story in his own phraseology. But literary students were not quite satisfied with this, for something of the charm was lost. It was like putting the stories from the Bible or from Homer into our modern speech; the form of the ancient narrative was marred. So when Dr. Lane's scholarly translation was published, it was eagerly welcomed. The Arabic stories are, however, extremely simple in form. They are told as a child tells an experience of his own, with many "ands" and "thens" to connect the different items of the tale. Lane's edition was at the same time too elaborate and too much abridged to be an equivalent, and there were students of Arabic literature who were better satisfied with the full translations.

There is in the detailed versions much which to us seems tiresome and unnecessary. The poetical selections, especially, have little interest for modem readers, although these impromptu verses were an essential feature of the original tales. An abridged edition being required for school use, it has been my purpose to select the most famous and characteristic of the stories and to give to them something of the original flavor. This was the more practicable because they were first cast in a form natural to oral story-telling. As, however, some of the tales are evidently much later in their origin than those that belong to the original collection, I have given these—notably "Aladdin" and "Ali Baba"—a more modem phrasing.

There are in the different versions many inconsistencies, but these are in the main unimportant. Proper names, especially, are given in various forms; I have endeavored to select the form most common in general literature. It is a small matter also whether we say "Gulnare" or "Jullnar," "Giafar" or "Jaafar," "Moslems" or "Mussulmans," "caliph" or "khalifah"; but it is in the highest degree desirable that we recognize the place held in literature by this "immortal fragment," as Burton calls it. Fortunately when we have once read of Sindbad and Agib and Bedreddin the magic begins to work, and we do not need wise scholars to tell us that here is a wonderful realm of enchantment into which every reader with a spark of imagination in his nature will gladly enter.

Kate Douglas Wiggin (*The Arabian Nights*):

Little excuse is needed, perhaps, for any fresh selection from the famous "Tales of a Thousand and One Nights," provided it be representative enough, and worthy enough, to enlist a new army of youthful readers. Of the two hundred and sixty-four bewildering, unparalleled stories, the true lover can hardly spare one, yet there must always be favourites, even among these. We have chosen some of the most delightful, in our opinion; some, too, that chanced to appeal particularly to the genius of the artist. If, enticed by our choice and the beauty of the pictures, we manage to attract a few thousand more true lovers to the fountain-book, we shall have served our humble turn. The only real danger lies in neglecting it, in rearing a child who does not know it and has never fallen under its spell.

You remember Maimoune, in the story of Prince Camaralzaman, and what she said to Danhasch, the genie who had just arrived from the farthest limits of China? "Be sure thou tellest me nothing but what is true or I shall clip thy wings!" This is what the modern child sometimes says to the genies of literature, and his own wings are too often clipped in consequence.

"The Empire of the Fairies is no more.
Reason has banished them from ev'ry shore;
Steam has outstripped their dragons and their cars,
Gas has eclipsed their glow-worms and their stars."

Edouard Laboulaye says in his introduction to *Nouveaux Contes Bleus*: "Mothers who love your children, do not set them too soon to the study of history; let them dream while they are young. Do not close the soul to the first breath of poetry. Nothing affrights me so much as the reasonable, practical child who believes in nothing that he cannot touch. These sages of ten years are, at twenty, dullards, or what is still worse, egoists."

When a child has once read of Prince Agib, of Gulnare or Periezade, Sinbad or Codadad, in this or any other volume of its kind, the magic will have been instilled into the blood, for the Oriental flavour in the Arab tales is like nothing so much as magic. True enough they are a vast storehouse of information concerning the manners and the customs, the spirit and the life of the Moslem East (and the youthful reader does not have to study Lane's learned footnotes to imbibe all this), but beyond and above the knowledge of history and geography thus gained, there comes something finer and subtler as well as something more vital. The scene is Indian, Egyptian, Arabian, Persian; but Bagdad and Balsora, Grand Cairo, the silver Tigris, and the blooming gardens of Damascus, though they can be found indeed on the map, live much more truly in that enchanted realm that rises o'er "the foam of perilous seas in faery lands forlorn." What craft can sail those perilous seas like the book that has been called a great three-decker to carry tired people to Islands of the Blest? "The immortal fragment," says Sir Richard Burton, who perhaps knew the Arabian Nights as did no other European, "will never be superseded in the infallible judgment of childhood. The marvellous imaginativeness of the Tales produces an insensible brightness of mind and an increase of fancy-power, making one dream that behind them lies the new and unseen, the strange and unexpected—in fact, all the glamour of the unknown."

It would be a delightful task to any boy or girl to begin at the beginning and read the first English version of these famous stories, made from the collection of M. Galland, Professor of Arabic in the Royal College of Paris. The fact that they had passed from Arabic into French and from French into English did not prevent their instantaneous popularity. This was in 1704 or thereabouts, and the world was not so busy as it is nowadays, or young men would not have gathered in the middle of the night under M. Galland's window and cried: *"0 vous, qui savez de si jolis contes, et qui les racontez si bien, racontez nous en un!"*

You can also read them in Scott's edition or in Lane's (both of which, but chiefly the former, we have used as the foundation of our text), while your elders—philologists or Orientalists—are studying the complete versions of John Payne or Sir Richard

Burton. You may leave the wiseacres to wonder which were told in China or India, Arabia or Persia, and whether the first manuscript dates back to 1450 or earlier.

We, like many other editors, have shortened the stories here and there, omitting some of the tedious repetitions that crept in from time to time when Arabian story-tellers were adding to the text to suit their purposes.

Mr. Andrew Lang says amusingly that he has left out of his special versions "all the pieces that are suitable only for Arabs and old gentlemen," and we have done the same; but we have taken no undue liberties. We have removed no genies nor magicians, however terrible; have cut out no base deed of Vizier nor noble deed of Sultan; have diminished the size of no roc's egg, nor omitted any single allusion to the great and only Haroun Alraschid. Caliph of Bagdad, Commander of the Faithful, who must have been a great inspirer of good stories.

Enter into this "treasure house of pleasant things," then, and make yourself at home in the golden palaces, the gem-studded caves, the bewildering gardens. Sit by its mysterious fountains, hear the plash of its gleaming cascades, unearth its magic lamps and talismans, behold its ensorcelled princes and princesses.

Nowhere in the whole realm of literature will you find such a Marvel, such a Wonder, such a Nonesuch of a book; nowhere will you find impossibilities so real and so convincing; nowhere but in what Henley calls:

"... that blessed brief
Of what is gallantest and best
In all the full-shelved Libraries of Romance.
The Book of rocs,
Sandalwood, ivory, turbans, ambergris,
Cream-tarts, and lettered apes, and Calenders,
And ghouls, and genies—O so huge
They might have overed the tall Minster Tower,
Hands down, as schoolboys take a post;
In truth the Book of Camaralzaman,
Schemselnihar and Sinbad, Scheherezade
The peerless, Bedreddin, Badroulbadour,
Cairo and Serendib and Candahar,
And Caspian, and the dim, terrific bulk—
Ice-ribbed, fiend-visited, isled in spells and storms—

Of Kaf . . . That centre of miracles
The sole, unparalleled Arabian Nights."

Frances Jenkins Olcott (*The Arabian Nights*):

Of all the folk-literature adapted for children, none is more richly imaginative, warm in colour, and full of varied adventures than the "Arabian Nights' Entertainments," for which reason a volume of selections from the same should be in every child's own library.

This edition of selected tales edited for young people is based on the version of the Oriental scholar, Edward William Lane. His translation from the Cairo text, although it is the standard, classic household version for adults, may not be given unexpurgated to children as it contains much that is unfit for them to read. It has, however, great educational values, the chief of which lie in its epic treatment, so characteristic of primitive people; in its thrilling adventures, related with convincing details; and in its dignified style, resembling that of Bible narrative. Its educational values are increased by Lane's painting, as with a large, free brush, desert scenes, and life in the great Oriental cities; and in his depicting Eastern customs and religious beliefs which control the "faithful" Mohammedan's daily actions.

The tales abound in Genii with their heads in the clouds, their feet resting upon the earth, their heads like domes, their hands like winnowing-forks, their legs like masts, their mouths like caverns, their nostrils like trumpets, their eyes resembling lamps, and hair dust-coloured and dishevelled; and with damsels as beautiful as the shining moon, with eyes like those of gazelles, cheeks like anemonies, mouths like the seal of Solomon, and figures like the waving branch. The stories also describe Oriental cities crowned with domes and minarets, subterranean abodes, flying Genii; and verdant gardens in which are flowing rivers, blossoming flowers, and trees full of birds proclaiming the praises of Allah the One, the Omnipotent.

The pages of the original Lane edition are illustrated with the delicate drawings of William Harvey, who in true Oriental spirit depicts the buildings, costumes and life of Mohammedans. As it is almost impossible to reproduce satisfactorily these old engravings, coloured illustrations are here substituted for the Harvey drawings.

Several of the stories included will be new to most children. Of these are "The Story of the City of Brass," which relates the search for bottled Genii; "The Adventures of Hassan of Balsora," which describes the wonders of the enchanted Islands of Wak Wak, and the humorous story of "Caliph the Fisherman."

Two stories, "Aladdin" and "Ali Baba," are not included in the Cairo text, and as an edition for children of the Arabian Nights would be incomplete without these tales I have added them, editing the versions of Jonathan Scott, translated from the French of Galland.

In rendering these stories I have retained the original language as far as possible. The familiar forms of proper names are given instead of Lane's more accurate but uninteresting transliterations, and English equivalents have been substituted for some Arabic words. Long sentences are shortened, tedious conversations condensed, and lengthy stories broken into chapters. Those parts of the stories unsuitable for children are removed, which in a few cases necessitates slight changes in the plots. I have, however, conscientiously tried to preserve the original matter, and the genius and customs of the Arabians, making only such alterations as the interests of the children demand.

The Training of the Imagination

by James Rhoades

When first I was requested to read a paper before this august assembly, my heart, I confess, so failed me, that nothing seemed less attainable than the possession of sufficient courage for the task. "And yet," said I to myself, "can it really be that, after so many years' experience, you have positively nothing to say upon the art which you profess?" For many days echo answered "Nothing," and I wandered about forlorn and miserable, and "trembling like a guilty thing surprised." I tried indeed to console myself with the reflection that it is not necessary to practical success that one should have a theory to advance, or feel strongly about other people's theories; that, after all, it may be better to belong to the great company of dumb workers, better to dig in the gold mines of silence than the silver mines of speech; that there was nothing to blush for, if I had always proceeded upon instinct, and, without preconceived ideas, had trusted in emergencies to draw my inspiration from the "hour and the" boy. But the straws of comfort which I thus gleaned, ended, I felt, but in mildewed ears, from which could be obtained no solid sustenance. My despair deepened: I turned to Bradshaw, either with a view to flight, or in the hope that he might guide me to a parliamentary train—of thought; but all was useless: "there is nothing for it," I moaned, "but to throw off the mask, to confess that all these years you have been an impostor, concealing your ignorance, with more or less success, from the British parent and confiding chiefs; better, far better, not to go down into the vale of years with a lie upon your lips, but having nothing to say upon the subject of Education, to come forward like a man and say it." With thus much then, by way of introduction, I proceed to say my "nothing" upon the importance of training the Imagination, satisfied that the subject itself is a great and pressing one, and that, though the best service one can render may be to make original remarks and throw new light upon obscure problems, the next best is to clear the ground for others, and earn their heartfelt gratitudes by forestalling all the platitudes.

First, however, let me premise that if in the present paper I shall seem to ignore all the advantages that are resulting from the increase of the materials of knowledge on the one hand, and the organization of the means of acquiring it on the other, and if I seem to pose in some degree as a sceptic, or conservative, it is not that I am blind to "the blessed light of Science," although I may have ceased to believe that it brings the millennium in its train, but because I have a latent fear, that where the gain is so enormous in one direction, there must be a corresponding loss in another, that the very completeness of our success may involve our failure, that we may be so absorbed in perfecting the means and instruments of Education as to mistake them for the end.

What, then, is the somewhat reactionary attitude which I venture to assume? It is this, that there is a possible bad side, a very real peril, in all this increase of learning, multiplication of subjects, systematization of methods, cataclysm of school-books—all the machinery which has been brought into play to aid us in our wild desire to *know,* and to reduce the art of teaching to an exact science. I hope you will agree with me that the object of education is not to know, but to live. True it is that Browning's "Grammarian" is held up for admiration, because he "determined not to live, but know:" but then he existed in the dawn of the revival of learning, and was an exceptional case, an intellectual pioneer; accordingly, if you remember, he suffered from baldness, tussis, calculus, and died, first from the waist down, and then altogether, at a comparatively early period of his career. My contention then is that we are in danger of trusting too much to books and systems, too little to the living influence of mind on mind; too much to rapidity of learning, too little to development of power; that we are in danger of organizing the soul out of education, of making it mechanical and therefore barren; of a tendency to look to the accumulation of facts as an adequate result, though they may lie like lead in the brain that bears them; in a word, of confounding the mere capacity for housing mental goods with the growth of the vital powers conferred by education.

What is the meaning of all this feverish desire to know? What do we gain by it ourselves that we should so labour to roll the mighty snowball on, a still increasing burden to every generation? Is it a morbid appetite of the brain, destined to grow with that which feeds it, till it leaves us a race of monsters at last, with bulbous heads and puny frames? If so, why all this haste to inoculate our children with the deadly lymph? Or is it a veritable boon?—a thing which makes us happier in its possession, or better? Not *all* the wise, at any rate, have thought so. "He that increaseth knowledge increaseth sorrow," said a paragon of ancient learning. "Ah! years may come, and years may bring the truth that is not bliss," said Clough. "Knowledge comes, but wisdom lingers," says Tennyson. "Nothing else will give you any comfort, when you come to lie here," said the dying Scott, but he was not referring to his intellectual store. It does not, however, require the authority of such opinions as these to persuade us that knowledge may bring sorrow, that she is not synonymous with bliss, that she is quite a distinct personage from Wisdom, and that she is of no service to us on our dying-bed. When we meet a learned man, it does not necessarily occur to us to wish to be like him, or to have him as our companion upon a walking-tour: it does not follow that he is also an admirable, or even a truly educated, man. Learning, therefore, cannot be the "summum bonum" of life: I doubt if it be a "bonum" at all, except when regarded as a means to a "melius." Knowledge, indeed, or rather the material of knowledge, I conceive to be simply mental food—that which, taken in moderation and duly digested, enables the mind to live and think and grow in its own proper sphere, of which more anon. To make knowledge an end in itself, to live for it, is surely as blind an act of folly as to live for eating; excess in the one case being followed by the same results as in the other. "Inconveniences," says Sir Thomas Elyot, "always doe happen by ingurgitation and excessive feedinges," and this is no less true of the mind than of the body. I do not know that a well-informed man, as such, is more worthy of regard than a well-fed man. The brain, indeed, is a nobler organ than the stomach, but on that very account is the less to be excused for indulging in repletion. The temptation, I confess, is greater, because in the former case the banquet stands ever spread before our eyes, and is, unhappily, as indestructible as the widow's meal and oil. Only think what would become of us if the physical food, by which our bodies subsist, instead of being consumed by the eater, were passed on intact by every generation to the next, with the superadded hoards of all the ages, the earth's productive power meanwhile increasing year by year, beneath the unflagging hand of Science, till, as Comus says, "She should be quite surcharged by her own weight, and strangled with her waste fertility"! Should we then attempt to eat it up, or even store it? Should we not rather pull down our barns, and build smaller, and make bonfires of what they would not hold? And yet, with regard to knowledge, the very opposite of this is what we do. We store the whole religiously, and that, though not twice alone, as with the bees in Virgil, but scores of times in every year, is the teeming produce gathered in. And then we put a fearful pressure on ourselves and others to gorge of it as much as ever we can hold.

I believe, if the truth were known, men would be astonished at the small amount of learning with which a high degree of culture is compatible. In a moment of enthusiasm I ventured once to tell my English set that if they could really master the Ninth book of *Paradise Lost,* so as to rise to the height of its great argument, and incorporate all its beauties in themselves, they would at one blow, by virtue of that alone become highly cultivated men; and surely so they would: more, and more various learning might raise them to the same height by different paths, but could hardly raise them higher. (A parent afterwards told me that his son went home, and so buried himself in the book that food and sleep that day had no attractions for him. Next morning, I need hardly say, the difference in his appearance was remarkable: he had outgrown all his intellectual clothes.) Yes, I am more and more convinced, it is not quantity so much that tells, as quality and thoroughness of digestion. Now digestion, to be thorough, must have time, and, to be worth much, must get done by natural means; and therefore I doubt whether our annotated school-texts, though excellent in themselves, are altogether wholesome, where every mouthful almost of learning is assisted by its own peculiar little pepsine pill of comment. This improved system of aids may indeed be necessary to meet the increased pressure of requirement from without; still, it does not follow that we are gainers on the whole. But to return to the question of amount. To myself personally, as an exception to the rule that opposites attract, a very well-informed person is an object of terror. His mind seems to be so full of facts that you cannot, as it were, see the wood for the trees; there is no room for perspective, no lawns and glades for pleasure and repose, no vistas through which to view some towering hill or elevated temple; everything in that crowded space seems of the same value; he speaks with no more awe of King Lear than of the last

Cobden prize essay; he has swallowed them both with the same ease, and got the facts safe into his pouch; but he has no time to ruminate, because he must still be swallowing; nor does he seem to know what even Macbeth, with Banquo's murderers then at work, found leisure to remember, that good digestion must wait on appetite, if health is to follow both.

Shakspeare himself, it seems,—I quote from a recent review in the *Spectator,*—"despite all that the commentators, doctors, ornithologists, entomologists, botanists, and other specialists find, or pretend to find, in his Work, was anything but a man of learning. He knew 'small Latin and less Greek,' and had but a smattering of French. Even of English literature, other than what was contemporary, he was no profound student, though he seems to have read with some attention both Chaucer and the older chroniclers... But his mind assimilated the very marrow of the books he read." Now, if a mind like Shakspear's can be built up on such a slender basis, it follows that quantity in learning is not a matter of the first importance. I speak under correction, but I suppose that Newton, with the stock of learning which he carried "into the silent land," could not now-a-days win the senior wranglership. And yet are any of our senior wranglers his equals hitherto? It was something other than his learning, then, that made Newton Newton. You may say that, both in his case and in Shakspeare's, it was genius, and that this is incommunicable. It may be so; and yet can we get much nearer to a definition of genius than by naming it the power of assimilating in remarkable degree all the influences which radiate from the universe and man—the power of so sympathising and identifying itself with all outside it, that the mind becomes surcharged at last, and needs must out with its burden and disclose its secret, whether in song, or by the revelations of science, or on canvass, or with the sculptor's tool?

Of course, in such supreme degree, this power can be but for a few; but I maintain that intellects of ordinary strength can be raised by education, not indeed to create, as does the artist, but through his creations to reach and to enjoy the same exalted pleasure, and absorb it into their systems; that, till such absorption begins, there is no true education; that at this stage, and not before, the mind begins to live and move and have its being. Here then first opens before the student's eyes what I mean by the world of imagination. If any one is still awake, I will try to describe it further.

Were I asked to sum up in a few words, my ideal of education, I should define it as the art of revealing to the young or ignorant the existence of an atmosphere above them and about them of which they do not, or but dimly, dream; of teaching them to desire and aspire to it; of unlocking for them one or more of all its myriad gates—a world of thought and law, of marvels and of mysteries, of moral beauty and ideal truth, beginning haply where they had hoped all need of effort ended; a glorious region, out of which conceit or sloth may keep them, but which besets them always and on every side, and yet soars far above the foggy belt of highest man's attainment. To give them the upward glance, the initiated eye; to let in "the light that never was on sea or land"; to show that "heaven lies about us," not only "in our infancy"; to help dispel those "shades of the prison-house" which never ought to "close about the growing boy,"—if to do this for one benighted mind thou hast been able, "thou art among the best of the" pedagogues; if for many and many, "thou art the non-pareil."

I care not what the subject we may teach: Of all I ever heard of, there is none that does not open upwards to this paradise. For the lover of science what a moment must it be when he first feels the beggarly elements are mastered, that henceforth he is not merely soiling hands and clothes with acids and with fossils, but projecting himself in spirit into the unknown past and reading the secrets of the eternal Master-builder; that here is a realm of inexhaustible delights, through which his mind may roam at pleasure, winged and free!

To the lover of mathematics what scent and taste of ocean when he, too, dares to push from shore into those "strange seas of thought" where Newton voyaged "alone"! He need not make discovery of continent or island, like the great ones that have gone before; but wafted with a breath of the same spirit, in their track he sails: his bark is nobly rigged; and, though the light breeze may not bear him far from land, he can lie at anchor where he will, assured that, whether cutting through the billows or becalmed upon their surface, he, at any rate, is rocked upon the bosom of eternal truth. Not even to the poet, I am told, is imagination a more present help than to the mathematician (and I can well believe it, for my own knowledge of mathematics exists almost entirely in imagination), nor is there any subject, I suppose, in which a boy, who has been furnished by nature with the requisite canoe, can sooner or with more delight paddle out into the great unknown.

For the lover of music, again, what a door is opened, when his enjoyment first ceases to be little more than a mere sensual pleasure, a soft shampooing of the soul, and he gets a glimpse into the mysteries of sound, and feels his whole being swayed and thrilled by those mighty laws that seem to lie at the foundation of the universe, and to pervade it; whose operation reaches from the whirring of an insect's wings to the rolling of the thunder, and from lower still to higher still, beyond the ear of man, from the gurgling of the sap within the tree to the rhythmic order and orbits of the stars! Yes,—

"Painter and poet are proud on the artist-list enrolled:

"But here is the finger of God, a flash of the will that can,
Existent behind all laws, that made them, and lo they are!

And I know not if, save in this, such gift be allowed to man,
That out of three sounds he frame, not a fourth sound, but a star.

"Consider it well; each tone of our scale in itself is nought;
It is everywhere in the world—loud, soft, and all is said;
Give it to me to use! I mix it with two in my thought,
And there! Ye have heard and seen: consider, and bow the head!"

When, I say, this door is first opened, the wonder of the vision overpowers him, and he knows himself a pigmy, and burns his comic songs and begins to read Mendelssohn's letters, and thinks no more of the pattern of his trousers.

And then, again, to the lover of history what a field is there to roam in and hold living converse, like Landor, with the dead!—But, lest your patience fail, I will imagine myself interrupted by an objection: "Yes," you may say, "all very fine. To the lover of this and the lover of that the revelation may come easily; but how to make lovers of those who are not?" That is the question; and, if I could have answered it satisfactorily, I should not have kept you so long in doubt as to the discovery.

But first, with regard to literature, what is the nature of the ideal realm to which, through its medium, the mind may rise? It seems to me that, the use of language being to convey thoughts and emotions, the chief end of learning any language is to gain admission to those treasures, and that this, therefore, should be the main educational aim with regard to language. Words are symbols, just as coins are; and, when we speak of words as coined and current, we imply that in themselves they are mere counters, representing, but not constituting, some form of real wealth and power. I do not say, of course, that words have no further value—they have—but this is secondary, and curious, perhaps, rather than elevating or inspiring. They may be treated, as coins are by the coin-collector, as objects of historical and antiquarian interest; but this is purely an incidental and accessory, not an inherent and essential use. To treat them as if it were otherwise, seems as little reasonable as to amass money chiefly for the purpose of numismatic research. To utilise cash, indeed, we must know the value of each piece; but we need not be acquainted with the date, the reign, the mint where it was struck, the depreciation caused by man's clipping or the wear and tear of time. Not that the comparison is absolutely just. Words are of infinitely greater variety than coins, and of infinitely deeper interest, being in themselves, as it were, fossil fragments of the human life of ages, and yet having laws of development and growth, which raise them almost to the level of living things. Still, I say, that the beauty of the laws of language is a lower thing than literary beauty, which depends partly on the thought to be expressed and partly on the fitness of the words which express it; just as beauty of physical frame and feature is a lower thing than that subtle combination of physical with spiritual which we term "expression of countenance." A higher thing than the beauty either of words, or of thought clothed in words, is the pure thought itself, which is thus conveyed to us through the senses, just as what we call soul or spirit is a higher thing than either physical beauty or beauty of expression. But, as through the expression of a man's countenance we can often read his thoughts and feelings, and even his character too, in proportion as it has power to imprint itself on the face, so through the medium of literary expression can we arrive at the writer's thought and feeling, in proportion as they have power to stamp their likeness on the language that he uses. In literature, therefore, the region that lies open to the initiated rises heaven over heaven. There is the lowest of the three, that which deals with language pure and simple, and is mainly of historical and antiquarian interest; there is the second, the heaven of incarnate thought, as it were—thought clothed in language; and, thirdly, there is the heaven of disembodied thought, to which from the last is but a moment's flight, and from which we must descend as often as we would communicate it to our fellows.

What, then, is the point in all these studies where routine ends and imagination begins?—Exactly where interest, where pleasure begins: where the mind, instead of being led blindly in a groove, begins to act upon its own account, like a living thing, and, having taken and assimilated food, anon desires more, and roams abroad to find it, and makes that glorious region her home. To grow by any study, we must admire, be touched, perceive the latent charm, not merely be able to dissect and reconstruct the outer framework. The works of nature or of man must awaken in us emotions corresponding to the divine or human feeling or purpose that inspired them. Then, and not till then, the mind begins to feel her wings, and tries her first flight into the ideal world—

> *"What poets feel not, when they make,*
> *A pleasure in creating,*
> *The world in its turn will not take*
> *Pleasure in contemplating."*

And equally true it is that, till the world feels that pleasure, it cannot rise to the empyreal region from which the poet sang.

Now, to take a passage from Horace referring to M. Atilius Regulus:

"(Atqui) And yet (sciebat) he was all the time aware (quæ) what things (barbarus tortor) the foreign executioner (pararet) was preparing (sibi) for his entertainment," and so on,—may be a very creditable translation for a member of the Lower Fifth; and, when you have further discovered that he knows why "pararet" is subjunctive and imperfect, and that "sibi" does not refer to the executioner, a man may flatter himself that the lesson has been well learned and so it has. But, for all that, the main thing is yet to do. The learner with rope and axe, mechanically, has climbed high enough to get some view of the outward form; he cannot see the passionate feeling of mingled pity and admiration which inspired, moulded, lies behind, that form; his imagination is not touched; he little dreams that a man might have much ado to keep his voice steady while reading the concluding stanzas of that ode aloud; he has not the faintest notion that they are electric and alive for ever by virtue of their inherent and undying charm. Little by little then, even from the earliest stages, to open their eyes to these wonders ought, surely, to be our aim, more gradually of course in teaching a dead language, most rapidly in teaching English; to reveal the splendours of the realm of genius, till at last the marvel of it strikes them, and they feel "like some watcher of the skies when a new planet swims into his ken," and are amazed at the magic touch which can take a handful of common words, such as "blow," "winter," "wind," "unkind," "ingratitude," and, with a sprinkling of conjunctions, prepositions, and pronouns transform them into a thing of perfect beauty and immortal breath. Is this the wealth we desire to have for ourselves and our children—the wealth, for instance, of the soul of Shakspeare, or the possession and intimate knowledge of the coins that express, and the caskets that contain it? Which is best to live by? Which would help us most from *ennui,* disappointment, faint-hearted ness, the spirit of "Blow, blow, thou winter wind," and of "As you like it" altogether, with its precious "implaister of content," or an accurate acquaintance with the etymology of the words, the metrical, peculiarities, redundant pronouns, etc.? I may be mistaken, but I never can persuade myself that Shakspeare would have passed high in a Civil Service examination-paper on one of his own plays; and yet, I suppose, it would be our ambition to produce minds that should approximate to Shakspeare's mind, rather than to that of Wren's most successful pupil.

But this approximation is only to be attained by seeing, admiring, loving. In his preface to the second edition of Lyrical Ballads, Wordsworth says:—"We have no knowledge that is, no general principles drawn from the contemplation of particular facts—but what has been built up by pleasure, and exists in us by pleasure alone"; and again taking an extreme instance to illustrate his point, "However painful may be the objects, with which the anatomist's knowledge is connected, he feels that his knowledge is pleasure; and when he has no pleasure, he has no knowledge."

It is clear then that the teacher, unless he be a blind leader of the blind, must first possess enthusiasm for the beautiful himself. If this be so, and if he do not hide his light under a bushel, the battle is half won already. He must lose no chance of rousing his pupil's sympathy for what is worthy of admiration. It often surprises me to find how boys are awed by a master's feeling for what at present is above their reach. Personally, whenever in the lesson I can find a peg to hang a poem on, I always hang it; and I have hardly ever felt myself unrewarded. When stirred himself by the pathos or the grandeur of some expression, thought, or deed, that occurs in the course of teaching boys, and when the ripple in his own mind spreads, and sends a thrill of emotion, or perhaps only of awakening interest into theirs, it is then, I think, a master feels that for a moment he has touched "the shining table-lands" of his profession.

Another aid, and one by no means to be despised, is the possession and cultivation of a sense of humour. It would seem to be characteristic of the same mind to appreciate the beauty of ideas in just proportion and harmonious relation to each other, and the absurdity of the same ideas when distorted or brought into incongruous juxtaposition. The exercise of this sense, no less than of the other, compels the mind to form a picture for itself, accompanied by pleasurable emotion; and what is this but setting the imagination to work, though in topsy-turvy fashion? Nay, in such a case, imagination plays a double part, since it is only by instantaneous comparison with ideal fitness and proportion that it can grasp in full force the grotesqueness of their contraries. It is like a man who, gazing out of window, sees passing by some "phantom of delight," destined indeed to be "a *moment's* ornament"—the next, by a faulty pane of glass caricatured, and grimacing in unconscious deformity.

Yes, there is no other entrance to the realm of which I speak but through the folding gates of pleasure and of wonder. It might almost be said that, in teaching, the three main faults to be avoided were:—1st, dulness; 2nd, dulness; 3rd, dulness. The things that boys will forgive their masters well nigh surpass men's understanding. Be irascible, impatient, abusive, sarcastic, exacting, severe; make bad puns even, and they will forgive you till 70 times 7, but not, if you be dull: "out, out, vile spot!" or all the perfumes of Arabia will not sweeten your teaching in the nostrils of boys. Heavens and earth, what a world to be dull in! and what a place and opportunity to choose, with a score or so of minds about you, each as dry and porous as a sponge, and ready to drink in the beauty and the wonder, if you could but show it them! You may say such heights are altogether above them, out of reach of the younger at any rate; that it is but teaching them to fly badly, when they should be learning to walk well; that they lack imaginative power. There I join issue: boys seem to me of imagination almost compact: look at their unquestioning faith, look at the boldness of their sanguine guesses, outsoaring the highest flight of man's conjecture, look at their devotion to the inseparable novel; see how, during a sermon, the moment such words as "I remember once" herald the coming story, all coughing, fidgeting, and shuffling ceases, back into pocket flies the surreptitious watch! you can almost hear a pin lie still upon the floor. No, they have imagination, and to spare; what it needs is wakening and directing. But this cannot be done by insisting on the mastery of mere facts alone. The most conscientious drudgery, though it may strengthen the character, will not refine the mind. You may set men to dig through a mountain; and chip, chip, chip, into the darkness they will go; but they will not go far, unless they feel that they are working towards the air and light: you must let down shafts into the tunnel, and open heaven to them from above, or they will sicken soon and drop. So too must we irradiate the dreary chip, chip, chip, through fact and commentary with something of the breath and brightness of the open sky. "It is increasingly felt," says an accomplished scholar in the preface to a recent translation of Sophocles, "that a good translation is a commentary of the best kind." This is a hopeful sign; for this lets in the soul at once into the stiffened features of a dead language, attracts, illumines, stimulates.

One more practical hint occurs to me to offer, and then I have almost done. If so much depends upon the teacher's quickening and modulating power, it behoves him before all things to keep his own mind vigorous and in tune. Therefore, I would say, avoid unwholesome diet both of body and mind; avoid needless worry; do not open long blue envelopes just before a lesson; do not attempt to enter on an argument with your wife; above all do not put yourself at the mercy of your betters and wisers by reading them papers on educational subjects. These things are fatal to that equilibrium of nerve and temper, on which the success of a schoolmaster so largely depends.

Well, we started with the assumption that the end of Education was not to know, but live. It is only by the application of *ideas* to life that man's existence, even in the lowest sense, is rendered capable of improvement. So successful has the *idea* been in dealing with material problems, increasing man's outward happiness, and ensuring his triumph over nature, that the danger seems now to be lest he should pause here, and rest content with this meagre and barren victory. Barren it is, and meagre, because, in the stress of life's extremities, the material does not stand us in good stead: it turns out to be illusory, unsatisfying, not to be relied on. But in the realm of thought there is "hope that maketh not ashamed," consolation ever ready to sustain us, friends that cannot change or die. Therefore Matthew Arnold thinks that "the future of poetry is immense," and that "in poetry, as time goes on, our race will find a surer and ever surer stay."—Yes, for the ideal more and more turns out to be the only real. In religion, in politics, in the daily struggle of life, the more we lean on the material, the more we find it fail us. There is but one power that seems alike proportioned to our highest aspirations and our deepest needs. What it is, let Wordsworth answer:—

"Imagination is that sacred power,
Imagination lofty and refined;
'Tis hers to pluck the amaranthine flower
Of Faith, and round the sufferer's temples bind
Wreaths that endure affliction's heaviest shower,
And do not shrink from sorrow's keenest wind."

Selections from

Education Through Imagination

by Margaret McMillan

In one of his books on Education, Count Tolstoi dwells at some length on the fact that all governments, and nearly all great institutions, churches, societies, etc., concern themselves with questions affecting the training and instruction of the young. Governments—ecclesiastical and secular—are eager and anxious to influence the children. They, as it were, fling themselves upon the little ones, crying, "Thus and thus shalt thou do and learn—before it is too late." The child is no sooner out of his mother's arms than the solicitude of the Powers that Be attains its maximum. "Give me the child till he is seven," cried the priests of former centuries, "and you can do as you please with him (comparatively) afterwards." And in England to-day, School Attendance officers are instructed to advise parents to send their children of three and four to school, while the five year old is expected to attend regularly, as a matter of course. When we look abroad at neighbour nations we find that though the French and Germans do not possess such a system of infant schools as our own, yet these and other continental nations vie with us and each other in drilling, instructing, training, and influencing the young, that they multiply schools, and spend an ever increasing amount of thought and treasure in building up national systems of education. Thus at home and abroad Government, Churches, Sects, and Powers that Be, are determined to lay hands on the young and change them for better or worse!

But what is the nature of the change which all statesmen, politicians and sectarians desire to effect? Is it a very deep or very vital one? At the first blush it may appear so—especially to one who frequents public meetings or reads speeches by prominent "educationalists" in the newspapers. Much is made of the "religious question," and something of foreign competition, and the national place of the workers in the world market; but gradually as we listen and read popular speeches and articles the truth is borne home to us that the word "education" has a widely different meaning for different writers and speakers. It has become "popular" without on this account, becoming more than an empty symbol to many, and the very facility with which we use it does not tend to make us examine very closely or exhaustively its true meaning.

Now there are certain words that may very well have a work-a-day meaning and be used quite safely as work-a-day symbols. We all use the word "water," signifying in so doing a transparent, colourless, odourless liquid, good to drink, and which at a certain low temperature becomes ice, at a certain high temperature vapour. That is enough for ordinary purposes in the way of content. The chemist and physicist mean a great deal more than this when they think of "water"—but their knowledge is supplementary, a mere enlargement and development of the popular interpretation. But the popular content of the word "education" is not fixed. Far from being the nucleus of a complete content it signifies to thousands instruction in the three R's, or it may be a name signifying some vague scheme of drilling and discipline, whereby the children of the rising generation are to be benefited somehow. Olsen, of Denmark, found that of the public school children 100 per cent, of the boys and 100 per cent, of the girls had a good working content for the word "ball," only thirty per cent, of the boys had a good working content for the word "dew." There are probably few grown-up persons who have not a good working content for the words "money," "trade," "bread," "water," "interest," while the working content of even the average politician for the word "education" is not that held by Froebel, Herbart, Spencer, or even that of the ordinary person who has thought seriously on the subject.

Before going on to inquire what the content of the word "education" means to the psychologist and great teacher, let us look for a moment at the army of children who have to be "educated." Uniformity, the Ideal of the Indolent, has prevailed in the past, and yet in spite of the evil influences of a system that favoured an indolent sameness of treatment, nothing is more remarkable than the variety of type, environment, and experience which British children represent.

Here is the little London urchin who has graduated on the streets, whose wits are sharpened by manifold social experiences. Here the child of the rural midlands, familiar only with the fields and a few social usages and kinds of labour. Here is the son of the mill-hand of the northern counties, whose parents and elder brothers all work at the factory, and whose own life and future is bounded by a vista of tall chimneys and driving wheels. Here is the slum child with his hoard of sorrowful and evil impressions. And here the son of the fisher of the Western Isles, with his wealth of golden lore, locked in a strange tongue, his eyes keen to discern the changes of the sea, his ears full of its voices. What wealth and what poverty these represent. It is now well established that the mind of a school child is not, a tabula rasa—that he brings some mental possessions to school with him, and that this (so far as school is concerned) original endowment, is the starting point of all subsequent progress and achievement. How diverse is the original capital of these embryo citizens! Among the city children, many have never seen a grain-field, an oak, a lark. They know nothing of such common and necessary labours, as reaping, sowing, or sheep shearing. Of the country children, some have never seen a railway train. And of the young islanders, many have never seen a time-piece, or a tree. Yet original capital they all possess. And this original accumulation (whatever its nature) is the beginning of all—*the capital in iron.*

The more central and despotic the government the less does it take account, generally speaking, of these differences of original capital in individuals and groups or communities within the same nation. Not only have governments usually declined to consider the value of mental capital which is alien or unfamiliar, they have ignored peculiarly painful aspects of mental poverty when these presented themselves as stumbling-blocks in their way. "Give up all those foolish stories and customs," cried the alien who had no Gaelic, to the Highlanders; "they are remnants of superstition and barbarism or worse!" and the folk-lore and customs that were the mental food and expression of a vigorous race began to be told and practised, almost shamefacedly and in secret. Thus was original wealth ignored. "The catechism and the three R's must be learned," said the statesman and cleric, and so we gathered together half-fed neglected children into great classes, and made them form pot-hooks, and pray in a foul atmosphere and on empty stomachs. Thus was original poverty forgotten. Such forgetfulness is a denial of all the teachings of the great psychologists and teachers who have spent their energies and lives in discovering and making clear to us the great facts on which the whole fabric of pedagogical science now securely rests.

Briefly those essential facts are as follows:—The new-born child is (to quote Virchow) "a spinal creature" pure and simple. His activities consist in reflex movements, simple transformations of excitation. This spinal being cries, moves his limbs, his fingers, all his muscles. The ceaseless and innumerable movements which he makes during his waking hours are doubtless a series of aimless experiments. At about the age of three months or thereabout it is easy to distinguish from among them certain movements that are acquired and that have an aim.

There is a long apprenticeship for sounds as well as for movement. For months a child experiments with his vocal muscles, trying new sounds and repeating them for hours with extraordinary energy and perseverance. As he grows older he varies his self-educative efforts and extends his interests. From the fifth to the sixth month children begin, as Taine observes, to be ardent physicists and continue to carry on their investigations in this field with unabated zeal for about two years. Every cat, dog, and other animal becomes the object of their attention and experiments, and nurses during this epoch have a trying time. For the little one wants to touch and handle everything he sees. Physical investigation more than anything else, we are told, helps to teach us the actual value and right of the Imagination, so this period is one of rapid preparation. The child pursues his investigation all day long without interruption. In this way, out of the dim world of obscure general impressions, groups of perceptions emerge which will become by-and-bye the starting point of new efforts and achievements.

"The contents of the soul," says Lange, "assert themselves in the act of perception." The acquired perceptions represent the power of referring new things to the old. All that is within is taxed to find a point of contact, of union. Thus a little girl in a Board school looking for the first time at a fern called it a "pot of green feathers," and a younger child on seeing a Christmas tree for the first time, looked in amazement at the presents and ornaments in the branches and called them "birds!" In one of his books Daudet tells us of a little wood-savage reared in a charcoal burner's cabin who made collections of miscellaneous booty,—birds, moles, beetroot, potatoes. All these things were represented in his mind by the vague term "denraie." His little head "full of the rustling swarming nature around him like the whorl of the shell filled by the roar of the sea," his heart full of the emotion which every new form of booty could engender, he did not linger to make fine distinctions. Yet in such wide generalization there is the germ of abstraction. In the creation of names—and some children will go far towards creating a language which they use for a time, and then outgrow and cast aside—there is evidence of a tendency present already to which we own all the higher powers of the mind.

Later we shall have occasion to see that this urgent desire, or impulse to find expression is absent, or at least very languid, in some children. There is something worse than want of grammar, and that is the lack of energy, the overflowing energy which, during a short period, makes it necessary for some children to supplement the language which is too restricted for them. Meantime let us look for a moment at the same process of naming as it is carried on by older people.

"If we examine what is going on in us when we abstract one general idea from a sum of sensations and perceptions we find only a tendency, which provokes expression. The expressions may vary with the temperament and development. The artist acts what he feels—The dumb give us strange illustrations of primitive expression. But usually the tendency to expression is met by symbols or words. Every name is a dessicated and abbreviated relic of a primitive drama." Properly speaking we have no general ideas. We have tendencies to name—and names. "A name which we understand is a name linked to all the individual things which we can imagine or perceive, of a certain class, and linked only to things of that class. It corresponds then to the common and distinctive quality which constitutes the class and separates it from all others, and it corresponds only to this quality. In this way the word is its mental representative. It is the substitute of an experience which we cannot have. It takes the place of this experience. It is its equivalent.

We cannot perceive and maintain isolated in our minds general qualities. Nevertheless, in order to get beyond mere experience and seize the order and internal structure of the world, we must conceive general qualities. We go back, or rather take a roundabout path. We associate with every abstract and general quality one particular and complex little event, a sound, a figure easily imagined and reproduced. We make the association so exact and complete that henceforward the quality cannot be present or absent in things, without the name being present or absent also, and vice versa. In this way the general character of things comes within range of our experience; for the names which express them are themselves little experiences of sight, eyes and hearing, or vocal muscles or of internal images—that is to say, they are resurrections more or less clear of these experiences. A great difficulty is thus done away with. In a being whose life is only a diversified and continuous experience one can only find impressions—simple and complex, nothing more. With simple and complex impressions nature has simulated impressions which are neither the one nor the other, and which, being neither the one nor the other, appeared of necessity to be beyond the range of our mind as it is constituted."

Here we have the history of language. It takes its rise in the organism. After having experience through the senses of various things, a tendency is finally experienced which corresponds to what these things hold in common, to some general or abstract quality, and this tendency leads to the creation of a sign or substitute. Henceforward the intelligence is free from the slavery of dependence on mere sensation. "If we cannot transcend experience," said Tyndall, "we can at least carry it a long way from its origin." We get a considerable way from its origin even in the elementary schools, for there we find charts, maps, as well as pictures. Arithmetic is taught only for a little while by means of objects. Figures take the place of objects; and by-and-bye letters take the place of figures, in short, substitutes for experiences are found which enable us to deal with them in quite a new way. "When you wish to learn Geography," said a Russian lady to her little son "the servant will take you where you wish to go." Progress consists in this—that in time the pupil is able to do without the servant—to do without the journey even.

To be sure the journey *back* to experience is taken often and openly. More especially by the young. The child reveals naively the origin of all his thoughts, as for example did Céeile the child heroine of Daudet's book 'Jack,' who driving home one evening through the woodlands, looked down on her native village and exclaimed softly, "That is Nazareth." Any lonely scene bathed in sunset light recalled to her the 'pious stories' she had heard. But the pious stories themselves were made intelligible only by experience. Nazareth was her own village touched with mystery.

Progress then is a journeying beyond "brute sensation," as the French call it. If good instruction has followed deep and rich experience the new does not awaken too much astonishment or too little interest—it is neither wondered at blankly, nor left unconsidered. But perhaps the greatest change effected by development and education is that witnessed in the realm of feeling. At first even the outermost limit of the child's moral consciousness is bounded by sensuous feeling. He sees not only in things but also in persons only their uses or attractiveness—mainly their uses to himself. "The water," said one young child, "is a thing for me to swim in." "A day," cried another, "is a thing for me to play in." And if questioned very closely about their feelings, to the persons dearest and nearest to him, a child could make no other answer than this. "I love them because they are good to me." But later, standing no longer in complete dependence on others he finds other motives than that of self-interest for attaching himself even to strangers. He judges the actions and character of men he has never seen and that do not touch, even indirectly, his personal life. Self is withdrawn somewhat from the arena, or at least it figures no longer so constantly in the foreground. Once he beheld order slowly rising out of the chaos of impressions that besieged him from without, and now out of the chaos of the inner world a new order is disclosed.

Briefly this is the natural course of human education conditioned by the nature and law of the human mind.

Now as experience is the basis of all it is plain that we cannot ignore the child's own wealth or poverty of impressions when he arrives in school. If he possesses something of value, that something must not be ignored or cast aside. If his experience is all sordid the source of this impurity must be cleansed. To proceed in haste, to teach without considering the being who is to receive the teaching, is to lose time and pains.

Nor must we say, "Because this child is poor he must learn certain things that will help him in earning a living at a very early age. This is the practical course to take with him." Just as if a *poor* child's mind developed in a different order from that of other children! At a very early stage embryo of the most various orders are indistinguishable.

They vary greatly at a later stage. So in childhood the human mind progresses along the same path.

At first the child accepts all that is offered, food, stimuli, certain orders of experience.

Progress represents a growing independence (which never becomes complete) of "brute sensation." Mobile images take the place of experience. These become clearer with education. With education, too, they become more manageable and subject to the will. They may be shifted, selected, suppressed. Then higher orders of substitution come into existence, and may be possessed so completely that the image itself is in the way.

Education then, and even human progress itself, is largely if not mainly a development and discipline of the Imagination. This faculty, whose exercise is so often regarded as a kind of weakness, a yielding to temptation, is the most reliable of all as an indicator of the whole sum and progress of mental activities. Its nature, its discipline, its power, represents the growth, the discipline, the power of the whole mind. Thus we can learn little of anyone by asking "How much does he remember?" But if we knew what he has initiated, and in what degree and manner he can create and discover, and adapt, then all is told.

It is this last test which the children and youth of to-day are failing to pass satisfactorily. They learn to read, to write, to cipher, to sew, but not to initiate, to adapt, to use their resources freely. What can be the cause of this falling off?—for a falling off it is. No one can glance at the history and literature of England and doubt that at certain stages, if not at every stage, the creative imagination of the people was very far beyond the average of the most favoured nations. Her greatest men were unique in their sovereign possession of this faculty. Of Shakespeare it is said, "He had a complete imagination. His whole genius is in that word."—Bunyan's hell was more realistic than Dante's. And the industrial history of Britain certainly reveals no lack of creative minds, of inventive faculty!

It might seem that the very character of the race had changed! And yet there has been no fundamental change and in all human probability no serious loss. True, the more ordinary and mediocre types to-day may seem to gain a sudden prominence, while others, of more originality and initiative have gone under a cloud. The most vigorous natures have to consider the demand of the hour, the tide of public opinion. For years it has seemed as if England said to her artizans, "Now we have machinery, be as like machines yourselves as possible." But that hour has passed. Those words will be heard no more. We realize that the artizans of England must still be more than machinery. Only the old spirit lingers in the school—which is always well behind the social and industrial movement. Many a child still passes through his school life, using only a minimum of his powers, and expressing only a fraction of his personality. Nor is the case of the teacher always very different. He or she also has to conform too much. Until very recent days teachers had (not to create!) but to accept systems, and methods, as well as text-books, and reports almost without criticism! It is therefore very probable that if many to-day appear to have little imagination or adaptivity as compared with their fathers, this is not because of any depreciation and sudden bankruptcy in the race, but because of a temporary suspension of their most characteristic powers induced by routine methods of education and thought.

We are warned however that it is time to avoid mechanical methods in schools. Otherwise the great results of education will be sacrificed. Already the finger of the wise is pointed to the place where modern popular elementary education seems to break down.

It breaks down in the cultivation of the faculty which childhood is often said to possess in excess—Imagination.

Mind images, or memories are the re-presentation in us of absent things, or bye-gone experiences—the echoes of sensations of colour, odour, form, muscular impression, etc., in the organism. These may vary greatly in energy and precision in different persons. Such as they are they form the raw material of the creative faculty—the original material (if we may be permitted to speak of origins in connection with such a high development of physical energy as is implied in mind images) of all ideas and conceptions.

They are the material. But how are they used? By what are they used? Primarily by feeling, emotion, desire. It is emotion which puts into movement the resources of the human mind. Under the word Imagination we include then many factors. We presuppose the existence of sensations, of emotion, of images and their associations, the possibility of certain mental operations. In short, Imagination is not an elementary formation. It is not even a secondary one. It is called by Ribot a "tertiary formation." Yet this tells us little. What is Imagination? How is it distinguished from other faculties? Its salient characteristic is that it is *motor* in its origin and function. "Imagination," says Ribot, "is in the Intellectual order, what Will is in order of Movement. There is identity of development in the two cases. The establishment of willpower is slow, progressive, traversed by many slips and falls. The individual first becomes master of his muscles, and extends through them his empire over other things. The reflexes, the instinctive movements, are the material of higher movement. The Will has no patrimony of special movements proper to itself. It must associate and coordinate, since it dissociates in order to form new associations. It reigns by right of conquest, not by right of birth. In the same way, creative imagination does not spring into existence full-armed. Its materials are the *images* which are here the equivalents of muscular movements: it goes through a period of trials and essays: it is always, in the beginning, an imitation: it attains only gradually its complex forms. But there are still deeper analogies. The Imagination is subjective, personal, anthropocentric: its movement is from within outward towards an objectivation. Knowledge (that is to say intelligence in the restricted sense) has an inverse character, it is objective, impersonal, receives from without. For the creative imagination the inner world is the regulator. For the intelligence the outer world is the regulator. The world of my imagination is *my* world as opposed to the world of intelligence which is that of my fellows.... And what has been said of the Imagination may be repeated word for word in regard to the Will.

Futhermore Imagination and Will have a teleological character, are active in view of an end to be attained. One wills something with an end in view—it may be a frivolous or a great end. One invents always with an object in view, whether it be Napoleon who imagines a plan of campaign or a kitchen-maid who thinks of a new dish. Finally, there is an analogy between abortive imagination and abortive will. Under normal condition the will is expressed in an act. But in the case of the undecided, the vacillating, the act is not accomplished. The resolution cannot affirm itself in practice. The creative imagination also, in its complete form, tends towards exteriorisation—it affirms itself in a work which exists not only for the creator, but for everybody. But in the case of the mere dreamer, the imagination remains an internal thing only—it is not embodied in external action. Reveries correspond more or less to irresolution "*Dreamers* are the impotent members of the creative world."

The Imagination is trained and developed through exercise—as is the Will through the muscles. It is not most powerful where it seems to run riot. Its intensity and strength are greatest perhaps where it subjects itself to rules, even disappears, like a river flowing underground for awhile but emerging again into the light. The wild dreams and fantasies of early childhood do not proclaim the existence of great imaginative powers any more than do the restlessness of a little child proclaim him the possessor of immense muscular strength. Nevertheless in the earlier stages there must be freedom, simply because there is little power of subservience, direction and obedience. The early hymns of the Saxon barbarians were a concrete of exclamations. They thought of God, as of Odin, in a string of short passionate images. "They do not speak," writes Taine of them, "they sing, or rather cry out, each little verse of their poets breaks forth like a growl." There is no art, no natural talent for describing in order the different parts of an event or an object. The barbarians are in short like very young children. By uncouth movements and cries they advanced. They strove to express all in a cry—and the force of the internal impression, did not quickly unfold itself. Yet it began to unfold itself at last and was expressed in rude poems. Progress depends on this yielding to the initial and individual impulse whether the learner be a child at play, a barbarian making rude experiments, or a scientist engaged in original research.

The importance of free play as a factor in education lies also in this—that it is experimental. Pleasure in motion is not enough, the quickening sense of power must be there also. When this is felt children often become ambitious, bold, stern with themselves. Long ago the game of Kettles was popular among the girls and boys of the Highlands of Scotland. It was usually played with great rigour. "Everything is a fault," said the children beginning the game, "to push the stone twice, to touch the line, to hold the arms spread, to hop twice—everything is a fault." This rigour is not confined to movement plays. "The playful exercise of the recollective faculty" is, as Groos observes, "common in children." They perform mental feats unachievable by adults, such as learning by heart books of nursery rhymes, long poems, interminable stories. They will often burden their minds with lists of unconnected and meaningless words. Otto Pochler, at four, knew the birth and death of every German Kaiser from Charles the Great as well as of many poets and philosophers. There was no trace of vanity, no desire to show off in all this. We must explain these accomplishments and the rigour of kettle-players as the result of the desire to experiment playfully with one's own powers.

It is in this way (through exercise) that the mental as well as the physical powers develop. Children, and indeed all healthy adults, enjoy exercise, whether it be romping or the making of the multiplication table, golfing or the solving of a problem in mathematics. "Within the limits of the gymnasium," writes Mrs. Boole, "every position is permitted and encouraged which would be considered indecorous and disorderly in class." *So it should be mentally.* "Every mental faculty which a human being is to exercise at all, should be used, alternately, in 'work':—that is to say, in subservience to necessities or rules imposed from without, and in 're-creation'—that is by evolving its own laws from within. If this is not done the mental faculty flags: and 'work,' which should be truly mental, is done (ill or well) as a mere trick of brain and nerves, without any full or true mental action....If you wanted a boy to become a merely stupid, mechanical bankclerk, sure of never making a mistake, and also sure *not to* understand enough of what he is about to find out when his superiors are cheating the public and the shareholders, you should make him do his sums always one way *and forbid him to experiment on any day of the year.* If, on the contrary, you wished him to become a mere busy-body, clever at detecting errors in other people's sums, but incapable of keeping accounts properly, let him always do his sums by roundabout and "natural" methods. But if you want a capable arithmetican, able both to do the business he is paid for, and also to understand what is going on around him, and find out for himself how to do things which he was never shown, insist on rigid method during hours of work *and encourage very free and lawless experimentation occasionally.*"

Free experiment by children is troublesome to parents—more troublesome to teachers, but abhorrent to official administrators. The child who plays in fantastic ways with his own power, chooses his own subjects in drawing; improvises in defiance of all rules of time, melody, counter-point and fingering runs certainly the risk of becoming very troublesome. And yet without free experiment there is little to be done. The great genius—such as Mozart—persisted in taking his lessons merely as a guide and sometimes as a kind of interruption. Precocious artizans—such as Poncelet—experimented freely in their play hours, as indeed England's future artizans must be doing to-day if the Manual training centres and Technical colleges are ever to be of great value. What is learned at school comes in as material. Doubtless it was a deep consciousness of the possibilities of play that led Froebel to emphasize it, to engage the sympathies of teachers in it, to take part in games himself, and wistfully try to direct the young mind in its most important moments. And yet it is doubtful whether any extraneous help can help one in crucial moments—whether we had not better recognise at once that not assistance but freedom is wanted in play-time. A young child knows very well what movements rest him when he has been trying to sit still at table for a time, or hold, his chalk firmly. Just in the same way he will learn what movements and occupations rest him in the intervals of manual training, or geometry.

The only way to assist him appears to be to make the geometry or manual lesson as thorough, as little of a mere game or play as possible. This does not mean however, that the Imagination is to have no place in class. It means just the opposite. There is no real test or trial involved in any training where the creative faculty is allowed to remain dormant. In drawing, in arithmetic, in languages, the moment of integrating effort which means growth, is the moment when the child is obliged to fall back on his own resources, to discover his own method, to write his own original composition, to draw from his own memory.

Unfortunately we show tendencies now to interfere much in the "play," without making sufficient demands in the "work." The consequence is that the Imagination is crippled at both ends of the system. There is much surveillance in the playing ground—there is a great deal of surveillance too in the classroom. In neither place is any very serious effort made to develop very completely the highest power of the human mind. Some of the causes of this neglect are deep-rooted and cannot be discussed here. Others are obvious enough. In our large class-rooms and small playing grounds thousands of children are massed. In order to keep order there must be rules and surveillance. The situation is in some respects a new one, it is certainly fraught with new risks. Uniformity has become an ideal. In accepting it we are simply following the line of the least resistance.

Yet such languid acquiescence (for it is nothing more) is bound in the long run to have serious results. The motive power of the moral life is Will. The motive power of the intellectual world is Imagination. In virtue of his power to imagine or re-create through mental images, man sees the past, forecasts the future, and has made whatever advance has been ever made into the fields of the Unknown. We cannot give Imagination to another, but we may arrest its development; and where it is ignored or suppressed, all intellectual life must quickly decline and perish. Now, as of old, wherever for one reason or another there is no vision the people perish.

Emotion—"Emotion is the ferment without which there is no creation." Man, possessed only of intelligence, the power of remembering, associating, distinguishing and reasoning, would produce nothing. At most he would be but a very fine order of automaton.

So far are we from being mere automatons in childhood that most of us can look back to some day in early childhood when we received a new initiation into life, through emotion, "After thirty years," said Taine, "I can remember every detail of the theatre where I was taken for the first time. The pit seemed to me like a monstrous pit, all red and flaming, with myriad dark heads surging above its depths; below, to the left, was a narrow platform, where two men and a woman entered, gesticulated, went out and returned again....I was seven years old—I understood nothing; but the crimson velvet pit was so crowded, so gilt, so illuminated, that in a quarter of an hour I was quite intoxicated by the sight of it, and fell fast asleep." Most of us have some such bright-tinted picture on the horizon of memory—brighter than recent mind images, and more enduring because of the emotion which stirred us on the long-past day when we made them our own. It was emotion—wonder, curiosity, astonishment, etc., which fixed our attention, in the first place, and the emotion we now feel in remembering the object or event helps to keep its colours bright and permanent. Nor is it hard to trace the creative impulse in such emotion. The painter and the romancer find in such memories the material for much of their work. Those not specially gifted in the arts re-create the whole epoch of childhood in the light of them. And where does childhood get the subject-matter of all invention save in memories made clear and arresting through emotion?

Without emotion, then, no development of imagination is possible. Mental and moral development depends, not merely on the learning of the right things at the right time, but also on the experiencing of the right emotions. How can we know that these emotions have been experienced? Only by the fruits of them, present and obvious in creative work. Spontaneous child-inventions, such as child-words, drawings, games, etc., are reassuring. They are all so much evidence of the activity of creative imagination, of *emotional* life, as well as mental life. Joy is the mother of many of these creations—also, wonder and admiration. The germ of human sympathy, as well as of intellectual activity is hidden in that spontaneous creativeness—like the fruit in the flower.

Unfortunately, there are a great many children who, through misfortune, have little impulse to create anything. They need no new vocabulary. They invent few or no new games, and have not the smallest desire to draw anything. When the school door opens for these a great many new tools are provided. There are books, pictures, colours—a new vocabulary even. But all these things are mere husks; for the natural emotions have not yet been experienced that would stir the imagination and give meaning to them. We may bring pictures of woodland and meadow, hills and sea into the school-room, but what does the child who has never seen the hills or the sea care for these things? We may try to describe trees, sky, waterfalls, etc., but we cannot give anything that will even *appear* to take the place of an original sense-impression. Who can describe a *sound* to one who has never heard the rushing of water, the whisper of trees, the warbling of birds? Nothing avails here but experience.

But the deepest human emotions are those which have their origin in human relationships. The little child learns to know his mother's or nurse's face well, to recognise her quickly and, in this recognition, emotion plays so great a part that the familiar face becomes a kind of starting-point of all the widening sympathy and interest of life. The law of interest is acknowledged to be of the first importance in the revival of images. "Doubtless," said Ribot, "the law of the affective life, the law of interest is less precise than is the intellectual law of contiguity and of resemblance." And yet it is more intimately concerned with the revival of memories. We remember a multitude of things in connection with the face of the person who first cared for and tended us, any one of which would call up the others in a more or less complete reintegration. And why? Because the emotion of love animates all these, and binds them in a unity that could not otherwise be realised.

If early life gives little opportunity for the experience of preserving and stimulating emotions, a remarkable mental apathy is the result. "Unhappy the heart," said Tourgenieff, "that has not loved in youth."

The head mistress of a large school in Bradford found her girls strangely lacking in observation. The school had good reports always, earned full grant, and the girls sang, read, and even worked sums quite satisfactorily. They made excellent garments, and the discipline was excellent. Nevertheless the teacher—a little puzzled, as many have been before her, at the extraordinary mental apathy that may persist in children who learn their three R's very creditably—made some new tests.

The girls were questioned only about things they had seen often. The school door is painted red and surrounded by a coat of arms. Of thirty-eight girls only three had noticed that there was anything over the door. Some said the door was painted yellow, others said it was black. All had seen cows passing daily up the street to the slaughter-house. Questioned as to the shape of a cow's foot, some said it was "long," others that it was "flat." Only two out of thirty-eight noticed that it was cloven. Children do not often observe the sky. It seems to be almost the last thing even grown-up people look at carefully, unless they are afraid of a wetting. So it is not surprising the class has little notion of the shape of clouds, or even of the colour of the sky on fair and stormy days. It was startling to hear from one girl, however, that "the rainbow is mostly white and brown." Street boys are quick in finding their way about. But it appears that this faculty is not developed in all city children in congested areas. Several girls of twelve and thirteen, of average ability, who had not followed the various callings of the street, knew very little of the buildings within a few minutes' walk of their own homes. They could not tell where the Town Hall is, or the Post Office, or the Parish Church, though these important buildings are within a short distance actually of the side streets in which they live.

Forty-five children from Standard IV. were examined. These have all seen ducks very often, but only twenty-eight have noted that the feet are webbed. Questioned as to the colour of the sparrows that hop about the yard, two said that they are "yellow." A great many looked puzzled and could give no answer. Of the thirty-five children in Standard II. who were questioned, four said the sparrow has four legs, one said it has six. One said the common house fly has four wings—being obviously confused rather than enlightened by the object-lessons from dead insects in school. Many, indeed, forgot the names of the specimens in various boxes, or confused them, so that nine out of thirty-five said the bee was much bigger than the very large butterflies, which were the only specimens in school. Six declared that the sparrow is yellow, five said that it is red. One said the sparrow is white, and another that it has six legs (another case of intruding insects). Lessons in Kindergarten, though recent for these scholars, were not applied. Sixteen said that their playground, which is oblong, was a square. Some children affirmed that a man's arms are fastened to his neck. Questioned as to the position of the eyes of a horse, nine girls out of forty five professed ignorance. The majority looked puzzled. It may, of course, be argued that children profess ignorance and express themselves inaccurately at times about things of which they are in reality quite cognisant. But, generally speaking, the drawings of the girls corresponded very closely to their statements. Below is a memory drawing of a cow by a girl of eleven. It is obvious that she had no idea of position, even with regard to so conspicuous a feature as the eyes.

The teacher realizing that the emotional life of her pupils was languid, questioned them one day about the animal they were to draw. "Where does the cow live?" she asked with animation. But the children who had seen cows only on their way to the killing shed, and were not interested in their doings or habits, replied that "the cow lived in the slaughter house." Clearly it is not by animation on the part of a questioner that an emotional background may be provided.

Neither do mere object lessons in class provide it. In every school emotional life has to be more or less assumed. The class room is not the place where all can be done, and experienced. It is the place where what has been lived through can be put in order. If the emotional experience is quite wanting, or of a depressing order, the teaching and explanations, though never so well done, appear to be singularly futile. The writer has a number of memory drawings of objects seen in school by children who have never been in the country—or hardly ever. The drawings reveal a great deal, and perhaps the fact of *least* importance which they make plain is—that the children never had any drawing lessons.

In some of the drawings there is evidence of confusion—powerlessness to arrange even the few natural objects which have fallen within the scope of the child's observation. Not only do the contents of the insect boxes come forth in an unwarranted manner.—The plants also behave in the same way. The curves and tangents of stem and leaf begin to appear in the memory drawings of animals, as in the case of the girl, aged thirteen, who sends in the next illustration. The horns between the ears are plainly a reminiscence of the school plants, or, perhaps, of the brush drawing lesson.

Such a drawing, and others of a like nature (as, for example, that of a girl who draws the head of one animal on the body of another), remind us that the class-room has its limitations. It had its limitations in the days when it contained only books, slates, ink, and paper. And it has its limitations now, when it is furnished with bird-forms, butterflies, plants, and herbariums. In the mind of the child, on whom new forms are thrust without preparation and under artificial conditions, "the elements," to use Herbart's phrase, "still commingle with one another." There is no "clear antithesis of single things" to prevent this confusion, and pave the way for true association. But above all the deep emotional stimulus is lacking, which, wherever it exists moves like a living thing, through even the faultiest, clumsiest work.

Some teachers, realizing the hopelessness of labouring with those who have neither experienced the emotions, nor accumulated the mind-images necessary for any kind of integrating effort escape from the class-room with their pupils, and give them a holiday time with opportunities. Pestalozzi was not long in finding his way into the woods with his little flock. Salzman and many other German teachers took the road with their scholars. Bartholomai organized regular school journeys in the streets of Berlin, undeterred by the laughter and jeers of the crowd and the bitter complaints of the Philistines that "the children's clothes and shoes were being ruined." Herbart, being a private tutor, did not take flight with a large number of children to the annoyance of the populace. But he remarks that for every boy, the best companions are peasants, shepherds, hunters of every kind and their sons.

These poor drawings are residues of confused experiences. They, like the poverty of vocabulary, the lack of games, the general want of interest can be traced to the same cause—Dearth of clear and suitable mind-images and healthy emotions. The invention by grown-up persons of suitable plays, a stimulating manner on the part of the teacher, even a chance visit to the country will not make the loss good. The teaching of drawing and colour-work on rational lines will effect very little. The school lesson as we saw already always pre-supposes a great silent preparation on the part of every child—the preparation of the mind—not by the learning of lessons—but by experience, and even freedom in experiment or play. The formal lesson cannot feed the sources of the creative powers. The sources of creative energy are the country, with its life, its human relationships in labour, its occupations and its beauty. Tolstoi puts into a child's mouth the words, "Art is the expression of an inner force." And these words are true. The drawings of the slum children are saddening, not because they show a lack of manipulative skill, but because they betray all the languor and weakness of the inner life—the dimness of the original perception of which they are only the residue.

60058959R00098

Made in the USA
Columbia, SC
14 June 2019